SPPU New Syllabus

*A Book Of*

# ECONOMICS - II

## (Indian Economic Environment)

**F.Y.B.A. Economics (Semester - II)**
**New Syllabus as per CBCS Pattern,**
**June 2019**

**Dr. Deepak D. Shinde**
M.A., M.Phil, Ph. D.
Assistant Professor, HOD Economics, Sanskar Mandir Sanstha's,
Arts and Commerce College, Warje Malwadi,
Pune 58.



NIRALI PRAKASHAN
ADVANCEMENT OF KNOWLEDGE

N5144

**Economics - II** **ISBN 978-93-89686-47-0**

**First Edition : December 2019**



**Published By:**
**NIRALI PRAKASHAN**
Abhyudaya Pragati, 1312, Shivaji Nagar
Off J.M. Road, PUNE – 411005
Tel - (020) 25512336/37/39, Fax - (020) 25511379
Email : niralipune@pragationline.com

## ➢ DISTRIBUTION CENTRES

**PUNE**

**Nirali Prakashan** (For orders within Pune) : 119, Budhwar Peth, Jogeshwari Mandir Lane, Pune 411002, Maharashtra, Tel : (020) 2445 2044, Mobile : 9657703145
Email : niralilocal@pragationline.com

**Nirali Prakashan** (For orders outside Pune) : S. No. 28/27, Dhayari, Near Asian College Pune 411041
Tel : (020) 24690204; Mobile : 9657703143
Email : bookorder@pragationline.com

**MUMBAI**

**Nirali Prakashan** : 385, S.V.P. Road, Rasdhara Co-op. Hsg. Society Ltd., Girgaum, Mumbai 400004, Maharashtra;
Mobile : 9320129587 Tel : (022) 2385 6339 / 2386 9976,
Fax : (022) 2386 9976
Email : niralimumbai@pragationline.com

## ➢ DISTRIBUTION BRANCHES

**JALGAON**

**Nirali Prakashan** : 34, V. V. Golani Market, Navi Peth, Jalgaon 425001, Maharashtra, Tel : (0257) 222 0395, Mob : 94234 91860;
Email : niralijalgaon@pragationline.com

**KOLHAPUR**

**Nirali Prakashan** : New Mahadvar Road, Kedar Plaza, 1st Floor Opp. IDBI Bank, Kolhapur 416 012, Maharashtra. Mob : 9850046155;
Email : niralikolhapur@pragationline.com

**NAGPUR**

**Nirali Prakashan** : Above Maratha Mandir, Shop No. 3, First Floor, Rani Jhanshi Square, Sitabuldi, Nagpur 440012, Maharashtra
Tel : (0712) 254 7129;
Email : niralinagpur@pragationline.com

**DELHI**

**Nirali Prakashan** : 4593/15, Basement, Agarwal Lane, Ansari Road, Daryaganj Near Times of India Building, New Delhi 110002
Mob : 08505972553, Email : niralidelhi@pragationline.com

**BENGALURU**

**Nirali Prakashan** : Maitri Ground Floor, Jaya Apartments, No. 99, 6th Cross, 6th Main, Malleswaram, Bengaluru 560003, Karnataka;
Mob : 9449043034
Email: niralibangalore@pragationline.com

**Other Branches : Hyderabad, Chennai**



**niralipune@pragationline.com | www.pragationline.com**

**Also find us on f www.facebook.com/niralibooks**

# Preface ...

There was a consistent stagnation in some parts of Indian Economy till 1991. But after adoption of New Economic Reforms some stagnated parts experienced robust growth but some still lagged behind such as poverty, employment, population, living standard, price stability, agriculture etc. Moreover the New Economic Reforms accelerated the pace of economic disparity and regional imbalance more profoundly. In such scenario it is very much necessary to study Indian economy as a whole before and after 1991. In this respect the framers of this syllabus have kept a great vision regarding knowledge and inquisitiveness among students.

The Board of Studies, Pune University, Pune has framed a new syllabus for FYBA part-I "Indian Economic Environment" and this new revised syllabus is going to effect from June 2019. So in this respect I am very much glad to hand over this much awaited and needful book regarding "Indian Economic Environment" for concern students and teachers.

This book is written according to new revised syllabus where I have made a sincere attempt to satisfy the trust of students and teachers by providing needful information, meaningful definitions, updated facts and figures, problems and its solutions and government policies etc. This book divided into three units as per syllabus. While preparing this book I have made use of an authentic and current data and information from different sources related to Indian Economy.

This book is useful for students, teachers and various competitive examinations aspirants. I sincerely hope that the book in its present form will prove very useful for the readers. Suggestions for the improvements of the book will be warmly welcomed and duly acknowledged.

I express my sincere thanks to ***Mr. Dineshbhai Furia*** and ***Mr. Jignesh Furia*** of Nirali Prakashan, Pune for having published this book. A special thanks to ***Mr. Malik Shaikh, Mr. Prasad Chintakindi*** for their valuable contribution to this book.

Any suggestions from students and teachers for further improvement of this book shall be welcome.

**PUNE** **AUTHOR**

**December 2019**

# Syllabus ...

(New Syllabus from June 2019)

**F.Y.B.A. – SEMESTER – II**
**ECONOMICS - II**

| Semester 2 | | |
|---|---|---|
| **Unit 1** | **Service Sector Environment** | **12** |
| | 1.1 Role and Growth of Service Sector in Indian Economy | 02 |
| | 1.2 Challenges to Indian Service Sector – Business-based and Knowledge-based Sector, Education sector, Health sector, Insurance, Tourism, Banking | 06 |
| | 1.3 Recent Trends in Indian Service Sector – Digital Economy, E-Commerce, E-Finance | 04 |
| **Unit 2** | **Banking Environment** | **18** |
| | 2.1 Banking-Definition, Functions, Changing Structure of Banking in India-New | 08 |
| | 2.2 Bank Accounts-Types, Procedure and Operation of Accounts | 05 |
| | 2.3 Recent Trends in Indian Banking Environment-E-banking, E-Wallets, Bank Mergers and Amalgamations | 05 |
| **Unit 3** | **Overview of Indian Economy** | **18** |
| | 3.1 Challenges of Indian Economy- Poverty, Employment, Inequality, Informal sector | 09 |
| | 3.2 Policy Measures (Two-Three recent Programmes)- Poverty Alleviation Programmes; Employment Generation Programmers; Agriculture Development programmes, Skill Develoopment Programmes. | 09 |

***

# Contents ...



***

Unit **1** ...

# Service Sector Environment

***Contents ...***



## INTRODUCTION

Fisher (1935) and Colin Clark (1940) have divided the economy into primary sector, secondary sector and tertiary sector. The primary sector is the one which covers tangible goods in agriculture, forestry, fishing and hunting. The secondary sector includes mining, manufacturing and such activities as gas, electricity and water supply involving activities with a tangible product. The tertiary sector consists of trade and public services. But this is not a clear cut division on economic activities as economists change the activities in the list and also there is overlapping of economic activities. Later on the economic activities have been shifted from one sector to other sector. At present, the primary sector includes agriculture, forestry, animal, husbandry and fisheries, etc. The secondary sector activities incorporate mining, manufacturing, electricity, gas, water supply, construction etc. The service sector activities include trade, commerce, transport, communications, hotel and restaurant, banking and finance, health and education, tourism, share market, film industry, insurance, astrology industry, advertisement industry, sports, legal service, publishing industry, mass media, etc.,

Service sector, also known as the tertiary sector of the economy, is expanding at a faster rate. The services sector in the country has a major share in transforming the nation into a developed country. Service sector involves activities beginning from production of goods and services until it reaches the consumer. For the last 35 years, there has been a substantial shift from the primary and secondary sector to the service sector. Now it has become a largest sector of the economy.

The service sector forms the backbone of social and economic development of a region. It has emerged as the largest and fastest growing sector in the world economy, making higher contributions to the global output and employment. Its growth rate has been higher than that of agriculture and manufacturing sectors. Services account for more than 60 per cent of world GDP and the trade in services has grown more rapidly than merchandise trade since 1985. It is a large and the most dynamic part of the Indian economy both in terms of employment potential and contribution to national income. It covers a wide range of activities such as trading, transportation and communication, financial, real estate and business services, as well as community, social and personal services.

**Definition of Service Sector:**

According to **Williamson and Lindert (1980)** *"Services sector is defined more specifically to be the sector of production outside of agriculture and industry, and includes construction, trade, finance, real estate, private services, government, and sometimes transportation, etc."*

"Service sector includes all activities which people offer, their knowledge and time to improve productivity, performance, potential and sustainability and also known as advice, experience and discussion".

## 1.1 ROLE OF SERVICE SECTOR IN ECONOMIC DEVELOPMENT

In any country, economic development depends on the growth and evolution of the three sectors viz. agriculture, industry and service sector of the economy. However, in recent years the service sector is growing at a very fast rate in the developing countries and is contributing a major share in terms of output, income and employment. Even the productivity per worker is becoming higher in service sector when compared to agriculture and industrial sectors. Already the service sector is dominant in the developed countries. If agriculture sector is stagnant, new service activities are emerging and adding to the service sector making the economy to grow. Hence, service sector is playing a major role in economic development of any country.

**(i) Contribution to GDP:**

The share of total services sector in India's GDP (at constant prices) which is constituted by trade, hotels, transport, storage and communication, banking, insurance, real estate, community and personal services, but excluding construction increased from 28.5 per cent in 1950-51 to 31.8 per cent in 1970-71 and then finally to 54.3 per cent in 2018-19 (see table no 1.1). Among the major components of services sector, the share of transport, communication, trade, hotel, finance insurance, real estate, business services, public administration, defence, construction, etc. increased during 1950-51 to 2018-19 (see table no 1.2). Thus, it has been observed that the contribution of services sector in GDP of India has been increasing in considerable proportion and thereby it has proved to be a major sector among all the three sectors of the economy.

**(ii) Rapid Growth of Services Sector:**

The importance of services sector to Indian economy can also be traced from its attainment of higher compound annual growth rate (CAGR). The CAGR of the services sector attained at 10 per cent for the period 2004-05 to 2011-12, has been found to be higher than the 8.6 per cent of CAGR of Gross Domestic Product (GDP) of India during the same period, which clearly indicates that the services sector has outgrown both the industry and agriculture sectors, showing its supremacy among all three sectors of the economy in recent years. Such rapid growth of the services sector has resulted in considerable changes in the GDP of the country.

**(iii) Higher Share of Services in GSDP:**

The services sector has been contributing towards the Gross State Domestic Product (GSDP) of different states and union territories (UTs) satisfactorily in recent years. A comparison of the shares of services in the GSDP of different states and union territories shows that the services sector is the dominant sector in most states of India. States and UTs such as Tripura, Nagaland, West Bengal, Mizoram, Maharashtra, Bihar, Tamil Nadu, Kerala, Delhi and Chandigarh have recorded a higher share of services sector to its GSDP which is again higher than all India shares of its services sector. Chandigarh with an 88.9 per cent share and Delhi with 84.3 per cent share top the list in 2017-18. This has resulted a horizontal spread of higher share of services sector in GSDP of a number of states.

**(iv) Employment Generation of Services Sector:**

The importance of services sector can also be realised from its contribution towards generation of employment in India. Although the primary sector (mainly agriculture) is the dominant employer followed by the services sector, the share of services sector has been increasing over the years and that of the primary sector has been decreasing. In 2017, there was 34 per cent employment created in the service sector. But the share of services in employment is roughly the share of services GVA for other countries such as USA (79%), China (56%), Japan (71%), Germany (72%), UK (81%), Brazil (69%), Mexico (61%) in 2017 implying that the services sector expansion in the recent decades has been unable to generate proportionate employment, especially in the formal sector. However, studies further reveal that the tertiary employment share has strong upward slopes in all the income quintiles covered both in urban and rural areas with higher income quintiles having higher share in each successive NSSO round. Thus tertiary employment growth is steadying moving from being an absorber of low income of labour to providers of high income jobs. State-wise, there are wide differences in the share in employment of different sectors in rural India. It is found that some north-eastern states like Sikkim, Tripura and Manipur have a high share of employment in the services sector and again some city states like Delhi have very high shares of employment in services 879 out of 1000 employed people. In urban India, the shares of employment in services in most of the states varied like 877 in Meghalaya, 833 in Assam, 826 in Chandigarh 787 in Jharkhand, 732 in Bihar, 711 in Kerala, 716 in Maharashtra, 743 in Rajasthan, 653 in Uttar Pradesh, 641 in Gujarat, 586 in Tamil Nadu and 683 in West Bengal out of 1000 employed people.

**(v) Contribution to India's Services Trade:**

The services sector is also playing an important role in raising the volume of exports in the country. Thus, India is moving towards a services-led export growth in recent years. During 2018, India's commercial exports growth rate was 10.7 per cent. As per BoP data of the RBI, India's services exports grew at a CAGR of 20.6 per cent during the period 2004-05 to 2010-11, compared to the 19.7 per cent CAGR of merchandise exports during the same period. If we enter into the details of services sector, CAGRs of financial services (29.2 per cent) were at higher level while that of software at 21 per cent was at lower level. Moreover, the overall openness of the economy reflected by total trade including services as a percentage of GDP showed a higher degree of openness at 55.0 per cent in 2011-12 compared to 25.4 per cent in 1997-98 and 38.1 per cent in 2004-05.

**(vi) Human Development:**

Services sector has a lot of contribution towards human development in our country. Accordingly, services sector has been rendering some valuable services, viz. health services, educational facilities, IT and IT enabled services (ITes), skill development, health, tourism, sports, cultural services, etc. which are largely responsible for human empowerment and improvement of quality of life of the people in general.

**(vii) Services Sector Growth and FDI Inflows**

Modest growth of services sector has made ample scope for the smooth inflow of FDI into the country. FDI also plays a major role in the dynamic growth of the services sector. On the positive side, at global level, medium term prospects for services are generally better than those manufacturing sector with international investment in the services sector expected to grow relatively faster. Moreover, many transnational companies, which some years ago were mainly focused on their home markets, are now pursuing their internationalization strategies involving ambitious investments abroad. Developing and transition economies particularly in Asia, are considered as most attractive destinations. Accordingly, India has been largely considered as favoured destination for increasing flow of FDI. Such FDI share of services was US$ 28264 and Total FDI Equity Inflows into India was US$ 44366 during 2018-19, the share of services in FDI inflows increases to 63.7 per cent.

**(viii) Development of Infrastructure and Communication Services:**

Services sector has also been playing an important role in developing expanding and management of infrastructure with a special emphasis on development of transportation and communication services. As a developing country, for India the importance of development of infrastructural facilities is quite high. The contribution of trade, hotels, transport, storage, communication and services related to broadcasting to the GDP at factor cost (at current prices) in India ranged from 8.2 per cent in 2006-07 to 7.8 per cent in 2017-18.

**(ix) Growth of IT and ITes:**

The services sector has also paved the way for a continuous growth of its IT and IT enabled services (ITeS) sector and thereby helping the economy of the country to attain higher growth both in terms of GDP share, employment, exports, etc. which has put India on the global map. The IT and ITeS sector of the country has developed an image of a young and resilient global knowledge power and has earned a brand identity in this sector. The IT and ITeS industry has four major sub-components : IT services, business process outsourcing (BPO), engineering services and research and development (R&D), and software products. This IT and ITeS sector has been generating considerable amount of revenues and employment in the economy. As per the Central Statistics Office (CSO), computer and related services with a share of 3.3 per cent in India's GDP grew by 14.4 per cent in 2013-14. As per NASSCOM's estimate, the revenue of the IT-BPM industry at US$119 billion grew by 12 per cent in 2014-15, while the export market at US$ 98 billion grew by 12.3 per cent over the previous year.

**(x) Development of Some Social Services:**

Services sector is also playing an important role in the development and expansion of some social services like sports, cultural services, etc. Sports promotes physical fitness and develops human personality which also plays an important role in national identity, community bonding and international bonding. Moreover, cultural activities or services include recreation and entertainment and radio and TV broadcasting besides other related cultural services. To meet the objective of preserving and promoting all forms of art and culture, a variety of activities are being undertaken by the Government of India. A total allocation of ₹ 3,555 crore was made to this sector during the Eleventh Plan. However, cultural activities are becoming increasingly important in the modern, post-industrial knowledge based economy.

**Growth of Services Sector in India:**

Services sector has been playing an important role in promoting overall enrichment of the society. Thus, services sector has attained a considerable size and dimension in its forms of activities and has been playing an important role in India. Because India is having a large size of population and presently enjoying the merit of population dividend in the form of growing proportion of working age population, the prospect and potential of the services sector in generating income and employment for its people is quite bright. Moreover, the growing volume of income and employment generated by services sector has been working as booster or major force for the other two sectors viz. industry and agriculture.

The services sector accounts for 54 per cent of India's Gross Value Added (GVA). Its growth rate moderated to 7.5 per cent in 2018-19 from 8.1 per cent in 2017-18. The segments that saw deceleration are tourism, trade, hotels, transport, communication and services related to broadcasting, public administration and defence. Financial, real estate and professional services category accelerated. An important finding is that India's services sector does not generate jobs in proportion to its share in GVA. This contrasts with the international experience. India received 10.6 million foreign tourists in 2018-19 compared to 10.4 million in 2017-18. Foreign exchange earnings from tourism in India stood at US$27.7 billion in 2018-19 compared to US$28.7 billion in 2017-18. Many of the high frequency indicators, such as bank credit to services sector, decelerated in 2018-19. However, the IT-BPM industry grew by 8.4 per cent in 2017-18 to US $ 167 billion and is estimated to have reached US $ 181 billion in 2018-19.

**Services Sector Contribution to Indian Economy:**

The services sector has been the most dynamic sector of the Indian economy, especially through the preceding ten years. Table 1.1 shows the changes that have been taking place in the services sector over the last few decades. It includes: (a) transport, communication and trade; (b) banking and insurance, real estate, dwellings and business services; and (c) public administration and defence and other services. From a low level of 30.3 per cent of GDP in 1950-51, the share of services increased to 58.2 per cent in 2011-12. Between 1950-51 and 2011-12, the share of services sector in GDP rose by only 27.40 percentage points, which is an increase of about 0.46 percentage points per annum. However, between 1990-91 and 2011-12, the share had increased by 15 percentage points, which is an increase of 0.75 percentage points per annum. Clearly, the rate of growth is significantly higher from 2000 onwards. In 2018-19, services sector share has been 54.3 percent but it is quite low from 2010-11.

**Table No. 1.1: Emerging Trends in Services Sector GDP (in per cent)**

| Year | Shares to GDP |
|---|---|
| 1950-51 | 30.3 |
| 1960-61 | 30.8 |
| 1970-71 | 33.8 |
| 1980-81 | 38.0 |
| 1990-91 | 42.7 |
| 2000-01 | 50.4 |
| 2010-11 | 57.7 |
| 2018-19 | 54.3 |

**Source:** Economic Survey Reports Various Years

**Performance of Services Sector in India:**

As per the provisional estimates for gross value added (GVA), services sector growth moderated in 2018-19 to 7.5 per cent rate from

8.1 per cent in 2017-18 (Following Table 1.2). This was due to a deceleration in the sub-sectors 'trade, hotels, transport, communication and broadcasting services' to 6.9 per cent and 'public administration and defence and others services' to 8.6 per cent in 2018-19. On the bright side, growth in the sub-sector 'financial services, real estate and professional services' picked up to 7.4 per cent in 2018-19 from 6.2 per cent in 2017-18. Despite the recent growth moderation, services sector growth continues to outperform agriculture and manufacturing sector growth, contributing more than 60 per cent to total GVA growth.

**Table 1.2: Services Sector Performance in India's GVA**

| Sectors | Share in GVA (%) | Growth (per cent) | | |
|---|---|---|---|---|
| | 2018-19 (P) | 2016-17 | 2017-18 | 2018-19 (P) |
| Total Services (excluding Construction | 54.3 | 8.4 | 8.1 | 7.5 |
| Trade, hotels, transport, communication and services related to broadcasting | 18.3 | 7.7 | 7.8 | 6.9 |
| Financial, real estate and professional services | 21.3 | 8.7 | 6.2 | 7.4 |
| Public administration, defence and other services | 14.7 | 9.2 | 11.9 | 8.6 |

**Source:** Economic Survey of India, 2018-19 P-Provisional

**Foreign Direct Investment Inflows into Services Sector:**

FDI equity inflows into the services sector 1 accounted for more than 60 per cent of the total FDI equity inflows into India. During 2018-19, FDI equity inflows into services sector fell by US $ 696 million or 1.3 per cent from the previous year to about US $ 28.26 billion, which is in line with the small decline witnessed in overall FDI inflows into India. This was driven by weaker FDI inflows into sub-sectors such as telecom, consultancy services, air and sea transport, which offset the strong inflows witnessed in education, retail trading and information and broadcasting.

**Table 1.3: FDI Equity Inflows into Services Sector (US$ million)**

| Services Sectors | 2016-17 | 2017-18 | 2018-19 |
|---|---|---|---|
| Financial, Business, Outsourcing, R&D, Courier, Tech. Testing and Analysis | 8,684 | 6,709 | 9,158 |
| Computer Software and Hardware | 3,652 | 6,153 | 6,415 |
| Trading | 2,338 | 4,348 | 4,462 |
| Telecommunications | 5,564 | 6,212 | 2,668 |
| Information and Broadcasting | 1,517 | 639 | 1,252 |
| Hotel and Tourism | 916 | 1,132 | 1,076 |
| Hospitals and Diagnostic Centers | 747 | 708 | 1,045 |
| Education | 160 | 286 | 777 |
| Retail Trading | 451 | 224 | 443 |
| Consultancy Services | 261 | 760 | 411 |
| Sea Transport | 735 | 1,051 | 279 |
| Air Transport | 83 | 629 | 191 |
| Agriculture Services | 76 | 110 | 88 |
| Total FDI Equity Inflows into Services | 25,185 | 28,960 | 28,264 |
| Total FDI Equity Inflows into India | 43,478 | 44,857 | 44,366 |
| Share of Services in Total FDI Inflows | 57.9 | 64.6 | 63.7 |

**Source:** Economic Survey of India, 2018-19.

However, the outlook and status of the services sector which had once fallen due to the global economic slow-down and financial crisis faced by the US, but the same sector has turned its heads towards its revival and growth once again. The growing opportunities in this sector have been generating employment to many across the nation and are also attracting FDIs for attaining success in future.

## 1.2 CHALLENGES TO INDIAN SERVICES SECTOR

### 1.2.1 Business Based and Knowledge Based Sector

The most important factor that has accelerated the process of economic evolution is the advancement of technology. Increasingly, traditional forces of production, land, labour, capital have become less important when compared with technology. Economists have termed this as the expansion of the production frontier. The source of technology science is rooted in knowledge. The Recent World Development Report highlights the importance of knowledge in the progress of a nations economy. While some developed countries through these way i.e. Great Britain took nearly 150 years. For the evolution of its industry, US did it in about 100 years, Japan was able to compress to about 40 years and Canada did it in 30 years.

In 1966, based on research undertaken by Industry Canada and the Business Development Bank of Canada, a definition of knowledge based industries (KBIs) was developed using the standard Industrial Classification (SIC). This has since been converted to the North American Industrial Classification system (NAICS). Since there was no single definition of a KBI, Industry Canada proposed the use of a two-tiered categorization of industries that would be appropriate for identifying industries as knowledge based.

### Meaning and Definition of Knowledge Based Industry (KBI):

The concept that supports creation of knowledge by organisational employees and helps and encourages them to transfer and better utilize their knowledge that is in line with company/organization goals.

Knowledge Based Companies (KBCs) are typically engaged in the areas such as software development, consultancy, pharmaceuticals, financial services, engineering services, biotechnology, etc. It creates highly competitive environment, the rapid change arising from technology advances and increasingly demanding requirements of their customer. Innovation is changing the market conditions.

India has a strong potential to develop a strong competitive advantage in knowledge based industries e.g. software industries.

**Characteristics of Knowledge Based Industries:**

1. To share information and knowledge.
2. To provide knowledge laws, barriers, taxes.
3. Knowledge enhanced products or services.
4. Price and value dependent knowledge.
5. Human capital knowledge.
6. Important for communication, social structure, cultural context.
7. To provide statistics knowledge.

### Broad Types of Knowledge Based Sector:

Generally four types of knowledge based sectors can be separated.

**1. Type a: The Technology Improving Knowledge Based Industry:**

The industry which purchases more outsourcing research activity and hires more knowledge based employees than average simultaneously, can be called as the technology improving knowledge industry.

The knowledge based employees are considered workers for improving the research result provided by research sector. This industrial sector purchases intermediate research services from the research industry more than average of all groups of industry and improves the proper goods or services by the in-house, professors, engineers. Output of this sector enjoys not only the integration of the outsourcing research activities but also improving the proper products to higher knowledge intensive goods or services. This means a typical transforming or improving industry i.e. communication equipment, electric measuring instruments and electronic apparatus, electronic parts, computers and related apparatus, household use electron and electric apparatus, heavy electric machine, precision machine, etc.

**2. Type b: The Outsourcing Depending Knowledge Industry:**

This type consists in hiring less number of knowledge based employees than average so that the purchased outsourcing knowledge can be used without much improvement comparatively. This industrial sector also purchases intermediate research services from the research industry more than average for all groups of industry but there is less value added process because there are less researchers or engineers in proper sector that the average of whole industry. This sector prefers buying research activities to investing the proper human resources in Research and Development. This sector consists of medicines, glass and glassware, chemical fertilizer, chemical fibers, etc.

**3. Type c: The Contents Creating Knowledge Industry:**

This type depends on less outsourcing knowledge than average but with more in-house. Professors, researches, engineers than average it can be more creative to produce the original contents of knowledge. This sector does not purchase average research service from the independent research industry but propels the knowledge creative activities by hiring researchers or engineers in the proper industry. There are numerous in-house researchers, professors or engineers. This sector consists of research, advertisement, investigation and information's services, water services, electric power supplies, other engineering and construction, etc.

**4. Type d: Three Clerks Industries:**

This industry is categorized as a ordinary industry and separated in 3 clerk's industries that is primary, secondary and tertiary industry. No specific label is given to this industry category.

All industries are, to some extent, dependent on knowledge inputs. However, some industries rely more on knowledge than others. The term knowledge based industries usually refers to those industries which are relatively intensive in their inputs of technology and human capital. While there are established methods for classifying manufacturing industries according to technology intensity capturing the right service sectors to help measure the impact of knowledge has proved more challenging reasons is limited availability and international comparability.

**Information Technology:**

Information Technology is known as the combination of three technologies, digital computing, data storage and ability to transmit digital signal through telecommunication network. Rapid change in semiconductors technology, information storage and networking, combined with advance in software has enabled new application, cost reduction and widespread diffusion of IT. The expanding array application makes IT more useful and further the expansion of IT.

Information is a resource which has no value until it is extracted, processed and utilized. Information Technology deals with information system, data storage, access, retrieval, analysis and intelligent, storage, presentation, and dissemination of information and also the processes and devices that enable all this to be done. IT affecting us as individual and as a society. IT stands firmly on hardware and software of a computer and telecommunication infrastructure.

Information Technology has spread very rapidly in India. But developed countries make more use of IT sector than India. Nowadays Indian people have increased the use of Information Technology. Following table shows that India had only 320 TV sets per 1000 population in 2009 as compared to other countries which was higher than India. It is against 990 in Japan, 980 in USA, 980 and 890 in Russian Federation and China respectively.

**Table 1.4: Various Countries Information in 2009**
**(Per 1000 population)**

| Country | Daily Newspaper | Television Sets | Telephone Main wires | Mobile | Broad Band | Internet Users |
|---|---|---|---|---|---|---|
| USA | 194 | 990 | 500 | 970 | 270 | 750 |
| UK | 289 | 980 | 540 | 1300 | 290 | 830 |
| France | 163 | 940 | 550 | 920 | 300 | 690 |
| Japan | 551 | 990 | 340 | 900 | 240 | 770 |
| Canada | 175 | 990 | 540 | 680 | 290 | 770 |
| Russia | 92 | 980 | 310 | 1624 | 90 | 420 |
| China | 74 | 890 | 230 | 560 | 1778 | 280 |
| India | 71 | 320 | 32 | 450 | 67 | 53 |

**Source:** World Bank, World Development indicates Russian federation

Above table shows that UK people used more internet services in all over world, i.e. 830 per 1000 population, 750 in USA, Japan 770, Canada 770, France 690, China 280, and India it was very low at 53 persons use the internet as per 1000 population. In 2009, Russia's population used more mobiles per 1000 population it is higher proportionate to other countries i.e. Russia 1625, UK 1300, USA 970, France 920, Japan 900, Canada 680, China 500 and India is 450 persons use mobile as per 1000 population. It clearly shows that, India much use of modern techniques with respect to IT.

**Table 1.5: Growth of Revenues of IT Market in India**

| Year | Revenue (₹ in Crore) | Revenue (US $ million) | As a percent of GDP |
|---|---|---|---|
| 1994-95 | 6,345 | 2,041 | 0.63 |
| 1998-99 | 25,307 | 6014 | 1.45 |
| 2000-01 | 56,592 | 12,410 | 2.66 |
| 2002-03 | 79,337 | 16,494 | 3.15 |
| 2009-10 | 3,45,761 | 73,100 | 6.1 |

**Source:** DattaSundaram, 67th Edition Indian Economy

Since 1994-95, IT revenues were ₹ 6,345 crores these are four times increased to ₹ 25,307 crores in 1998-99, which has also doubled to ₹56,592 crores, and again it was highly increased to ₹ 3,45,761 crores in 2009-10. As seen, the GDP contribution was 0.63 in 1994-95. It increased to 1.45 in 1998-99. In 2002-03, it has also increased from 2.60 to 3.15 per cent. Moreover, in 2009-10 information technology contribution to GDP was 6.1%. It clearly indicates that IT sectors contribution to GDP has increased in the given period.

**Software Exports:**

IT exports software and services. Export is important for country's development. It increases foreign reserves to country. Information technology sector came late in India. But its progress of last decade is unimagined. The table shows that export was ₹28,350 crores ($6217) in 2000-01. It reached at ₹ 2,69,630 crores ($ 60,591) in 2010-11. It is a good sign for Information Technology and for Indian government. Because IT sector is new sector, but it has increased export and consequently foreign reserves for India.

**Table 1.6: IT Software and Services Exports (₹ in crores)**

| Year | Export |
|---|---|
| 2000-01 | 28,350 |
| 2001-02 | 36,500 |
| 2002-03 | 46,420 |
| 2003-04 | 55,990 |
| 2004-05 | 79,404 |
| 2005-06 | 1,46,320 |
| 2006-07 | 1,41,356 |
| 2007-08 | 1,61,968 |
| 2008-09 | 2,12,877 |
| 2009-10 | 2,37,000 |
| 2010-11 | 2,69,630 |

**Source:** Indian Economy, Datta Sundaram, 67th Edition.

**Top Ten Software Companies in India:**

In a very short period, many software companies developed in India. It increase income, contribution to GDP, increase export and most importantly, employment. Many educated persons are getting jobs in software companies.

**Table 1.7: Top Ten Software Companies in India (₹ in Crore)**

| Rank | Companies | Revenue | | Growth Percentage |
|---|---|---|---|---|
| | | 2009-10 | 2010-11 | |
| 1 | TCS | 26,576 | 33,112 | 25 |
| 2 | Wipro | 21,949 | 24,899 | 13 |
| 3 | Infosys Technologies | 21,355 | 25,997 | 22 |
| 4 | Hewlett Packar India | 17,831 | 23227 | 30 |

| Rank | Companies | Revenue | | Growth Percentage |
|---|---|---|---|---|
| | | 2009-10 | 2010-11 | |
| 5 | Cognizant Technology Solutions | 15,646 | 21,393 | 37 |
| 6 | IBM India | 12,388 | 14,132 | 14 |
| 7 | HCL Info Systems | 11,956 | 14,111 | 02 |
| 8 | HCL Technologies | 10,983 | 12,137 | 28 |
| 9 | Ingram Micro India | 8,824 | 9,766 | 35 |
| 10 | Readington | 7,024 | 9,274 | 32 |
| | **Total** | **15,4532** | **1,88,048** | **21.7** |

**Source:** Indian Economy, Datta Sudaram, 67th Edition

TCS, Wipro, Infosys Technology are the leading companies in India whose revenue increase year to year. The table reveals that the top ten leading companies total revenue was ₹ 54,532 crores in 2009-10, further increased to ₹ 1,88,048 crores in 2010-11. It more increased in 2010-11 than 2009-10. Their growth rate was 21.7% in 2010-11.

### 1.2.2 Education Sector

Education is a critical input in human resource development and is essential for stimulation of economic growth of a country. The role of education in facilitation of social and economic progress is well recognized. It opens up opportunities leading to both individual and group entitlements. Education, in its broadest sense of development of youth, is most crucial input for empowering people with skills and knowledge and giving access to productive employment in future. Improvements in education are not expected to enhance efficiency but also improvement in the overall quality of life.

The provision of universal primary education is an effective anti-poverty measure that promotes equity. The poor are poor because they own very little assets of land, capital or skill. Land redistribution generates great social stress and opposition and capital to the poor would require large resources and may not be very effective if they are not imparted the skills to use this capital efficiency. Providing a skill is, however, not only possible but can be most effective. For this, the first step is primary education.

The 86th Constitutional Amendment of 2002 led to inclusion of a new Article 21-A in part III of the Constitution that made free and compulsory education to all children of 6 to 14 years of age. It is imperative to give good quality elementary education to all children in the age group of 6 to 14 years. Policies and Programmes in this direction are also necessary for honouring the country's commitment to the "Millennium Development Goals: and "Education for all" as well as commitment under the "National Common Minimum Programme (NCMP)" for increasing public expenditure on education to 6 percent of GDP and for universalizing elementary education at the national level.

In any nation, education is the basic necessity for the socio-economic development of the individuals and the society. In reality, only 20% of the population is educated in India. So, improved standard of education as first priority should be offered to the majority by the government authorities with sincere political will.

Education should be for the flowering of personality but not for the suppression of creativity or natural skill. In the globalized world, opportunities for the educated people are naturally ample in scope. As a result business process outsourcing (BPO) activities have increased competition in the world trade leading towards the production of quality goods and their easy availability everywhere in the world market. That is the way the world can be developed for peace, prosperity and progress by able and skilled men.

**Education System in India:**

The present education system in India mainly comprises of primary education, secondary education, senior secondary education and higher education. Elementary education consists of eight years of education. Each of secondary and senior secondary education consists of two years of education. Higher education in India starts after passing the higher secondary education or the 12$^{th}$ standard. Depending on the stream, doing graduation in India can take three to five years. Post graduate courses are generally of two to three years of duration. After completing post graduation, scope for doing research in various educational institutes also remains open. Despite all the efforts to develop the education system in India, access, equity and quality of education in India continue to haunt the policy-makers till now. This has mainly been due to the widespread poverty and various prejudices. The inability to check the drop out rates among the marginalized sections of the population is another cause of worry. However, the renewed emphasis in the education sector in the 11$^{th}$ five year plan and increased expenditure in both primary and higher education can act as palliatives for the Indian education system. After independence in the field of education, India started almost from a scratch and has since made significant progress in educational development. In the post-independence era, the progress in all types of education has been very impressive. The number of schools, colleges, universities has increased from 1950-51 till now. There has also been an explosion in student numbers. The enrolments in education have swelled from less than half a million in 1950-51 to about million in till. Such an educational explosion has been inevitable for the following reasons:

(i) Provision of educational facilities in the pre-independence period was very insignificant. Independence has created an unquenched thirst for knowledge resulting in an abnormal rise in social demand for education.

(ii) Building up a new socio-economic system after the end of colonial rule required large-scale manpower with varied skills, and so the government could not but expand the higher education system significantly.

(iii) The welfare state policies necessitated the expansion of the system horizontally, so that equity in all types of education could be promoted.

**Challenges to Education Sector:**

**1. Inclusion of People:**

The access to education among various groups such as castes, religions produces a dismally poor picture. While upper castes, Christians, Jains fare significantly higher than others, Muslims, SCs, STs rank way below national averages. The poor among all groups are the worst affected with abysmal enrolments. The rural-urban, female-male divide are staking too. Private un-aided universities are out of reach to majority of Indians.

**2. Fair Fees:**

Corrective measures should aim at spreading, strengthening of central, state university regulating the exorbitant fee charged by private universities. Providing credible financial assistance to economically weaker sections and encouraging higher education among SC, ST, Muslims is the need of the hour.

**3. Ranking:**

Rankings of our universities on Global, Asian level reflect the poor state of quality in education. Lack of quality coupled with poor access forms a vicious cycle for students.

**4. Improvement:**

Leveraging technology to provide massive online courses by IITs, IIMs can normalize quality levels. The challenges to educate are improving infrastructure, teacher-student ratio, strengthening regional language resources and building global network of academicians.

**5. Translate to Employment:**

Knowledge, skills should also translate into employability. Pursuing the objectives of National Skill Mission and encouraging industry-classroom relations can go a long way in making students industry ready and relevant.

**6. To Increase Quantity of Universities:**

We need more universities because we are more in number and present number of universities is too less. On 13$^{th}$ June, 2005 Government of India constituted a high level advisory body known as National Knowledge Commission (NKC) to advise the PM about the state of education in India and measures needed to reform this sector. It was headed by Sam Pitroda and submitted its report in November 2007. NKC has recommended setting up of 1500 universities by 2015 so that gross enrolment ratio increases to 15 percent. It has also called for establishing an Independent Regulatory Authority for Higher Education (IRAHE) to monitor the quality of overall higher education in India.

**7. Examination Reforms:**

Examination reforms, gradually shifting from the terminal, annual and semester examinations to regular and continuous assessment of student's performance in learning should be implemented. Many students are exam oriented and teacher are payment oriented hence it is a huge challenge to making reforms in examination system.

**8. High-tech Libraries:**

Our university libraries have a very good collection of books, but they are all in mess. A library must be online and conducive for serious study. Indian universities should concentrate more on providing quality education which is comparable to that of international standards. Moreover, majority of school libraries are not modernized particularly in rural areas.

**9. Internationalization of Higher Education:**

Globalization demands the integration of national economics with the free movement of goods, capital, labour and ideas. It has resulted in the perception of higher education as a commercial product governed by market forces and the principles of demand and supply. However, our higher education is totally unable to cope with international standards. Sub-standard higher education is creating problems of brain-drain as it fails to accommodate its talented students. Bearing in mind the consequences of globalization and the immigration of overseas students, it is essential to improve the standard of higher education in India.

**10. Quantitative Growth:**

Although there has been a noticeable increase in the number of universities, colleges, schools, students and teachers in education since independence, it is very low in relation to the size of the population and compared to developed nations. There are 684 universities in Japan, 2364 in USA and 330 in Germany. There are also insufficient infrastructural facilities to accommodate the growing needs of students and teachers of education in India.

**11. Quality Assurance:**

Qualitatively our higher education is very poor in respect to trained teachers, infrastructure, relevant programs, up-to-date interdisciplinary curriculum, research and evaluation.

**12. Research Work:**

The quality of higher education depends on intensive and extensive research programs. Today's higher education suffers from inferior research, which has no significance or contributory value to the field of education but is used instead of awarding degrees and certificates that lead to career promotion.

**13. Accountability:**

Lack of proper accountability curtails the standard of higher education. From managing bodies to teachers, students and parents, no one is truly accountable for their duties and responsibilities. There is no proper channel of assessment of their job responsibilities.

**14. Student Enrolment:**

Enrolment in higher education is still very low, accounting for only 7% of the total population compared to other developing nations like Indonesia, Brazil and Thailand where enrolment is 11%, 12% and 19% respectively. Moreover, the 1% pursuing higher education in India mostly belong to the higher and middle classes leaving the poor behind.

**15. Privatization:**

Privatization of higher education is a recent intervention as a result of globalization and has paved way for quantitative education. But the real challenge is to have quality control measures.

**16. Examination Reforms:**

The University Education Commission (1948-49) headed by Dr. S. Radhakrishnan stated that the single most important reform in higher education was the examination system. This system is now the home of blatant and widespread corruption, inefficiency, inaccuracy, rote learning, selective study, inflexibility and the active discouragement of innovative teaching, all of which have impact upon the quality of higher education.

**17. Inadequate Governance:**

Lack of openness and transparency in the governance of education from governmental level to university, college and school levels is acting as a bottleneck in the quality improvement of education and creating additional problems of the promotion of staff and fairness in administrative work.

**18. Curriculum:**

Higher education has failed to update its curriculum so that it can keep pace with globalization and techno-scientific developments. The outdated course content cannot and does not satisfy the needs of the present age but instead promotes unemployment, violence, superstition and fanaticism.

### 1.2.3 Health Sector

Good health is one of the basic human needs and worldwide recognized goal for faster socio-economic development. Health is an important aspect of human life. At present, it has also become an important aspect of any nation's health services and planning. Health is necessary for the realization of basic human needs and to attain the status of a better quality of life. Improving the quality of growth is an important goal of the development archetype in many developing countries. Better health, education, equal and wider job opportunities to all, trustworthy and transparent peoples intuition, sustainable and cleaner environment, dignity, self-esteem and life security, among others, are key manifestations of the quality of growth (WB, 2000).

The health of a nation is as essential component of development, vital to the nation's economic growth and internal stability. Assuring a minimum level of health-care to the population is a critical constituent of the development process. Since Independence, India has built up a vast health infrastructure and health personnel at primary, secondary and tertiary care in public, voluntary and private sectors.. For producing skilled human resources, a number of medical and paramedical institutions including Ayurveda, Yoga and Naturopathy, Unani, Siddha and Homeopathy (AYUSH) institutions have been set up.

Considerable achievements have been made over the last decades on efforts to improve health standards, such as improvement in life expectancy, reduction in child mortality, infant mortality and maternal mortality. Moreover, small pox and guinea worm have been eradicated and there is hope that poliomyelifs will be contained in the near future. Nevertheless, malnutrition affects a large proportion of children. An unacceptable high proportion of the population continues to suffer and die from new diseases that are emerging apart from continuing and new threats posed by the existing ones. Pregnancy and child birth related complications also contribute to the suffering and mortality. The strong link between poverty and ill health needs to the recognized. The onset of a long and expensive illness can drive the non-poor into poverty. Health creates immense stress even among those who are financially secure. High health-care costs can lead to entry into or exacerbation of poverty. The importance of public provisioning of quality health-care to enable access to affordable and reliable health services cannot be under underestimated. This is specially so in the context of preventing the from entering into poverty or in terms of reducing the suffering of those who are already below poverty line.

**Definition of Health:**

**According to WHO,** *"Health is a state of complete physical, mental and social well-being and not merely the absence of disease or infirmity".*

*"Health is a fundamental human right and attainment of the good health is an important worldwide social goal."*

**Health Sector and Economic Development:**

The health status is usually measured in terms of life expectancy at birth, infant mortality rate, fertility rate, crude birth rate and crude death rate. These indicators of health are determined by numerous factors such as per capita income, nutrition, housing, sanitation, safe drinking water, social infrastructure, health and medical care services provided by government, geographical climate, employment status, incidence of poverty (Reddy, 1994). It is in reality the quality of human health upon which the realization of life goals and objectives of a persona, the community or nation as a whole depends. Health is multi-dimensional phenomenon as it is both an end and means of development strategy. The relationship between health and development is mutually reinforcing while health contributes to economic development, economic development, in turn, tends to improve the health status of the population in a country. Health is also an important entitlement that enhances "capabilities" of the poor people leading to increase in "commodities" and further improvement in health status (Bloom, 2004). As investment on health increases, the productive capacity of the working population, and hence the level of income tends to rise and to that extent it contributes to a decline in the incidence of poverty (Reddy, 1994). With rapid improvement in health particularly of the poor, "vicious circle" of poverty can be converted into "virtuous circle" of prosperity (Mayer, 2000).

**Current Status of Health Sector:**

Health-care is India's one of the largest part of service sector in terms of revenue and employment and is expanding rapidly. During the 1990s, Indian health-care grew at annual compounded growth rate of 16%. Today, the total value of the sector is more than $34 billion. This translates to $34 per capita, or roughly 6% of GDP (India's Health Report 2012). By 2013, India's health-care sector is projected to grow to nearly $47 billion. Not only right to health-care has been recognized as a fundamental right in India, there are several international obligations for India to pursue 'access and equity' in this regard. The number of qualified doctors in the country is not sufficient for the growing requirements of Indian health-care. Moreover, rural "doctors to population" ratio is lower by 6 times as compared to urban areas. Around 74 percent of the graduate doctors in India work in urban settlements which account for only approximately one-fourth of the population. The countrywide distribution of these institutes is also skewed as 61 percent of the medical colleges are in the 6 states of Maharashtra, Karnataka, Kerala, Tamil Nadu, Andhra Pradesh and Pondicherry, while only 11 percent are in Bihar, Jharkhand, Orissa and West Bengal and the north-eastern states. In addition, India is a signatory to the Millennium Development Goals. MDGs represent the will of the world's nations to achieve development objectives by the year 2015. The importance of health-care in the MDGs is highlighted by the fact that providing health-care to all is the duty of the Central and State Governments. Unfortunately, India is far from providing a universal health-care coverage. Not only the improvements in health indicators have been slow, India lags far behind the world, including most developing countries and few least developed countries with respect to health indicators. In addition, within India there are large disparities amongst states in achieving health outcomes as well.

**Table 1.8: Health Indicators in India, 1951-2011**

| Indicator/Year | Birth Rate | Death Rate | Infant Mortality Rate | Maternal Mortality Ratio | Total Fertility Rate |
|---|---|---|---|---|---|
| 1951 | 40.8 | 25.1 | 148 | 1321 | 6 |
| 1961 | 38.7 | 20.6 | 129 | 1180 | 5.9 |
| 1971 | 36.9 | 14.9 | 120 | 853 | 5.2 |
| 1981 | 33.9 | 12.5 | 110 | 810 | 4.5 |
| 1991 | 29.5 | 9.8 | 80 | 424 | 3.6 |
| 2001 | 23.8 | 7.6 | 58 | 254 | 2.9 |
| 2011 | 21.7 | 6.9 | 44 | 197 | 2.5 |

**Source:** Book, Social Sector Development in India, by Deepak Shinde

Above Table 1.8 reveals that in the period from 1950 to 1971, India was engulfed in health deterioration as the values speak so high. The trend continued with the gradual decrease in the values of the health indicators. The annual growth rate after every ten years declined. Overall, the indicators have shown a declining trend with death rate decreased twice the birth rate, and same situation followed in other indicators as well. Thus, a dramatic change resulted in an improvement in the health sector.

**Challenges to Health:**

Changes in the health policy of a country have to be modified to the needs and prevailing situation. This is best explained when we discuss health reforms in India. India, with its unique demography, diversity, political and social systems and a recent leap in economy can be a challenge to the policy-makers. This section discusses the problems in health-care delivery in India and social, economic and political fundamentals for undertaking reforms in Indian health-care system. Problems in health-care delivery in India can be broadly divided into problems of inequality, socio-economic-political problems and unregulated growth of private health-care. The country has to deal with rising costs of health-care and growing expectations of the people. The challenge of quality of health services in remote rural regions has to be urgently met. Given the magnitude to the problem, we need to transform public health-care into an accountable, accessible and affordable system of quality services.

**1. Lack of Awareness:**

Lack of awareness is a problem which is faced in building access to health-care. Mass awareness is important since even if the treatment is free, unless the masses are educated and informed about the symptoms of the diseases, its repercussions and complications and finally the treatment available, there is no guarantee that people will avail these.

**2. Problems of Inequality:**

The effect of social and economic inequality on health is insightful. Poverty, which is a result of social and economic inequality in a society, is detrimental to the health of population. The outcome indicators of health i.e. mortality, morbidity and life expectancy are all directly influenced on population by inequality. There is no other country where the distribution of the health-care resources is abysmally unequal as in India. Only five other countries in the world are worse off than India regarding public health spending (Burundi, Myanmar, Pakistan, Sudan, and Combodia). The growing inequalities in health and health-care are taking its toll on the marginalized and socially disadvantaged population.

**3. Lack of Health Insurance:**

Low penetration causes further challenge towards access to health-care. With 75 percent of the Indian population paying for health-care services from their own pockets, it puts tremendous financial burden.

**4. Health System Strengthening:**

Important issues that the health systems must confront are lack of financial and material resources, health workforce issues and the stewardship challenge of implementing pro-equity health policies in a pluralistic environment. Epidemiological challenges like mental health, occupational health and other environment risks are yet to be put in place. There is a need for strengthening research infrastructure in the departments of community medicine in various institutes and to foster their partnerships with state health services.

**5. Problems and Issues in India's Health-care System:**

Key indices like maternal mortality rate and infant mortality rate are amongst the worst in the world. Unfortunately, this situation continues despite the government coming out with large scale initiatives. Out of pocket health expenditure caused due to lack of access to adequate public health-care is preventing a large section of population from climbing above the poverty line and pushing another large section back below the line. It needs to strengthen and expand the role of hospital accrediting agencies and make compliance mandatory for all health-care organizations. It needs to promote the development of specialist medical bodies that govern and oversee the practice of members of their speciality and issue periodic guidelines and clinical pathways to attain uniform practice. It needs to follow good advice about healthy lifestyles, eating habits and exercise and undergo periodic screening tests as appropriate. India suffers a large proportion of the disease burden of the world, which has been estimated to be more than its 16.8% share of the world's population. One of the vital elements in improving this situation is the need for a comprehensive and relevant evidence base that would equip India to take informed actions. A systematic assessment of recent health research output from India is not available. Without objective information about the current deficiencies and strengths in the health research output from India, it is difficult to plan substantial improvements in health research output that could enhance India's health status.

**6. Urban and Rural Areas:**

Lifestyle diseases due to changing working/living habits coupled with processed products have increased the instances of diabetes, cardio-vascular disorders and even cancer. Urban poor, due to poor physical infrastructure and awareness are leading to communicable and infectious diseases like tuberculosis, typhoid and other water borne diseases. The same can be said of villages with poor sanitation facilities.

**7. Political Will:**

India is a representative rather than a participatory democracy. Once the elections are over, the politicians who run the federal and state governments don't really need to go back to the electorate for every major decision. So, in the five years between one election and another there hardly are any means available to the citizens to voice their opinions on any decision taken by a government. In India, there are numerous gaps left by the government in the development process - sometimes by intention or due to lack of funds and sometimes due to lack of awareness. Most Indian politicians are hesitant to take harsh but healthy decisions as the politics of vote dominates the agenda. In the process, equality and social justice is an unavoidable subject. As in any reforms, a strong political will is the essence in health policy reforms too. The political will should be genuine and continual over a period of at least one to two decades to bring about any appreciable change in the system.

**8. Lack of Access to Health-care Services:**

It is hard to find any significant medical care. Diagnosis and treatment is just not accessible to hundreds of millions of Indians. *Public*

*Health in India: Issues and Challenges Sudha. S.R.* Volume-II, Issue-VI July 2016, 34 one of the biggest problems with health-care in India, specifically diagnostics, is that of the referrals or cut practice. It is the ethically questionable practice of sharing fees with professional colleagues, such as physicians or laboratories, in return for sent referrals. This problem is especially prevalent in diagnostics, with some doctors charging upto 70% of the pathology/radiology bills as a referral fee. Not only does this make quality health-care unaffordable for a huge number of patients, it also is inherently bad for the patient.

**9. Lack of Proper Health-care, both in Quantity and Quality:**

There is a serious lack of transparency. According to WHO, our per capita spending on health-care is in the bottom quartile amongst all countries. This has resulted in an appalling lack in basic government health-care infrastructure.

**10. Demand for Basic Primary Health-care and Infrastructure:**

India faces a growing need to fix its basic health concerns in the areas of HIV, malaria, tuberculosis, and diarrhoea. Additionally, children under five are born underweight and roughly 7% (compared to 0.8% in the US) of them die before their fifth birthday. Sadly, only a small percentage of the population has access to quality sanitation, which further exacerbates some key concerns above. One way to solve this problem is to address the infrastructure issue by standardizing diagnostic procedures, building rural clinics, and developing streamlined health IT systems and improving efficiency. The need for skilled medical graduates continues to grow, especially in rural areas which fail to attract new graduates because of financial reasons.

**11. Socio-Economic Problems:**

The state of economy has a direct effect on the state of health in a country. The health-care infrastructure directly depends on the economic strength. The recent changes in the economic policies had a definite effect on the health-care in India. In 1991, a program of economic policy reforms was launched with a view to attain macro-economic stability and higher rates of economic growth. Since India's economic reforms were launched in 1991, the Indian economy has sustained an annual average growth rate of over 6 per cent. In 2003-04, GDP growth was around 7.5 per cent. Health Sector policies in India have tended to stress on reducing population growth. Stabilizing growth of population is a matter of importance for a large country like India, as there are links between overall health status of population and population growth rate. In many of the Indian states where stabilization of population growth is not a priority, their health and social status is among the worst in the world. Diseases of poverty continue to affect more than half the population while environmental degradation; occupational hazards and new contagious diseases such as AIDS have a serious impact on the population. The phenomenon of urbanization has intensified problems of health-care. Illiteracy and lack of awareness amongst masses pose constant threat to the fabric of the society. This tilts the band of health in the wrong direction. Persistence of poverty in the social structure also complicates the health scene. The poor suffer excessively because of the double burden of traditional diseases as well as modern diseases that are caused by industrialization and rapid resource depletion. As a result, social inequalities persist and these affect the health of the poor more severely than it does the more well-heeled groups.

Thus, the challenges of health sector, but a problem of unnecessary and excessive diagnostic tests, a minor visit to the doctor Inadequate utilization of budgets, funds and resources by the government might be one of the main cause of poor health status of people. Some of the main problems faced by Indian health-care system are accessibility and affordability of quality health-care services and medicines to a large chunk of our population. Also lack of information and transparency are other major problems.

### 1.2.4 Insurance Sector

Insurance is an attractive option for investment. While most people recognize the risk hedging and tax saving potential of insurance, many are not aware of the advantages as an investment option as well. Insurance products yield more compared to regular investment options and this is besides the added incentives offered by insurers.

An insurance product cannot be compared with other insurance investment schemes for the simple reason that it offers financial protection from risks, something that is missing in non-insurance products. Insurance is a unique investment avenue that delivers sound returns in addition to protection. Designed to safeguard against losses suffered due to any unforeseen events, insurance provides the investor with unique sense of security that no other form of investment provides

Insurance also provides a safeguard in case of accidents or a drop in income after retirement. An accident or disability can be devastating; an insurance policy can lend timely support to the family in such times. It also comes as a great help when people retire.

**Definition of Insurance:** The definition of insurance are made by two types:

**Functional:** Insurance is a co-operative device to spread the loss caused by a particular risk over a number of persons who are exposed to it and who agree to insure themselves against the risk.

**Contractual (Justice Tindall):** Insurance is a contract in which a sum of money is paid to the insured consideration of insurer's incurring the risk of paying a large sum upon a given contingency.

## Types of Insurance:

### Life Insurance:

Life insurance is a written contract between the insured and the insurer, that provides for the payment of the assured sum on the date of the maturity of the contract or on the unfortunate death of the insured, whichever occurs earlier.

### General Insurance:

General Insurance or non-life insurance policies, including automobile and homeowners policies, provide payments depending on the loss from a particular financial event. General insurance typically comprises any insurance that is not determined to be life insurance. It also called Non-Life Insurance.

Health insurance, Business insurance, Automobile insurance, Fire insurance, Agricultural insurance, Credit insurance, Property insurance, Mortgage insurance, Pet insurance, Interest Rate insurance, Income Protection, etc. are the examples of General Insurance.

### Current Scenario of Insurance Business:

Globally, the share of life insurance business in total premium was 56.2%. However; the share of life insurance business for India was very high at 79.6% while the share of non-life insurance business was small at 20.4%. In life insurance business, India is ranked $11^{th}$ among the 88 countries, for which data is published by Swiss Re. India's share in global life insurance market was 2.00% during 2013. However, during 2013, the life insurance premium in India declined by 0.5% when global insurance premium increased by 0.7%. The Indian non-life insurance sector witnessed a growth of 4.1% in 2013. During the same period, the growth in global non-life premium was 2.3%. However, the share of Indian non-life premium in globally was lesser at 0.66% and India ranks 21st in global non-life insurance markets.

**Challenges for Insurance Business in India:**

The transition of the insurance industry from a public monopoly to a competitive environment now presents very interesting challenges, both to the new players and to the customer.

The benchmark of success of organization is not only determined by the rate of return but also by the quality of corporate governance. So good corporate governance practices should be followed by the companies as well as by the regulator.

Though LIC has done commendable work, there is still a great deal of scope for bringing in innovative products and distribution channels to tap insurance market.

Currently the product-market relationship is dominated by personalized selling rendered by tied agents. So the agents should be able to understand the complexity to assess the requirement of the populace and then only advice on the appropriate policy, which suits to the needs of the population. Also, companies will have to transform customer relationship management to the value-based client relationship.

Product development, Pricing mechanism and Technology management are the three sub-challenges of insurance sector. Insurance business is based on averages and spreading of risks. So, a flexible pricing structure for sustaining customer confidence and interest will be a challenging task before Indian issuers. The majority of insurance companies today are under tariff, that means insurance companies cannot price the product to suit the customer of customer group. The way to service customer is to segment the market and offer the correct product at the correct price to that market segment.

There is a huge untapped potential in India, which needs to be targeted. The distribution channel is a medium to reach the masses in urban, semi-urban and rural areas. So, the insurance companies should focus on pricing, distribution, risk management and investment decision-making.

The Indian insurance industry is currently facing severe headwinds owing to declining growth, rising costs, deteriorating distribution structure, stalled reforms.

**Measures to Counter the Challenges of Insurance Business in India:**

1. Direct marketing is one of the most successful channels of distribution in the developed economies. It is a great way to reach a large population. So the product should be sold through telemarketing or direct mail.
2. In the insurance business, cost control and ability to serve a large number of customers are crucial issues. So, modern technology is to be adopted to handle both the services effectively.
3. Today, customers are well-equipped with information. So insurance companies should reposition different products by changing customer attitudes.
4. The actuary should be required to attend minimum number of seminars called continuous professional development courses for financial control of the organisation.

### 1.2.5 Tourism Sector

Tourism today is emerging as a leading sector in the world and is now considered by some as the number one industry. Tourism industry is one of the largest segments under the service sector of the Indian economy. Tourism industry has strong relevance to economic development, cultural growth and national integration. The tourism industry has helped growth in other sectors as diverse as horticulture, handicraft, agriculture and construction. Tourism is the second largest foreign exchange earner in India. The tourism industry employs a large number of people, both skilled and unskilled. Hotels, travel agencies, transport including airlines benefit a lot from this industry. Tourism promotes national integration. It generates foreign exchange. It promotes cultural activities. Indian government's "Incredible India" tourism campaign and the information technology growth in India have been attracting millions of foreign tourists and business tourists to India.

**Tourism Policy of Government:**

Tourism in the country really came of age when the national policy began laying stress on the sector from the Third Five Year Plan during which the plan outlay for developing tourism was raised to ₹ 8.00 crores from a mere ₹ 1.58 crores during the Second Five Year Plan. Increasing public sector 19 outlays have been allocated to tourism during the successive five-year plans, ₹ 195 crores during the Sixth Plan and ₹ 345 crores during the Seventh Plan. The outlay for the Eighth Plan period has been fixed at a substantially higher level of ₹ 804.10 crores. A tourism policy was formulated and presented to Parliament for the first time only in November 1982. This policy was, unfortunately, more a statement of purpose than a concrete plan which was operationalized. The Sixth Plan document spelt out the objectives of tourism but it was far from being a comprehensive policy document or an action plan for the development or promotion of tourism in the country. The Seventh Plan outlined a long-term perspective on the development of tourism. It also advocated granting industry status to tourism, clear demarcation of the roles of the private and public sector and encouragement of investment in the public sector exploring tourism potential to support the local arts and handicrafts sector and to promote national integration. A significant milestone in the evolution of the tourism policy was the comprehensive report presented by the National Committee on Tourism in May 1988, which provided the basis of a long term perspective plan for tourism. During the Seventh Plan several new policy initiatives were taken to develop the tourism sector on an accelerated growth path. Tourism was accorded the status of an Industry. At present, 15 states and 3 Union Territories have declared tourism as an Industry. In addition, four states have declared hotels as an Industry. Consequently, a number of incentives have been provided to private entrepreneurs for investment in tourism activities. The future growth of tourism will be achieved through private initiative. The state can contribute to tourism by planning broad strategies of development, provision of fiscal and monetary incentives to catalyze private sector investments and devising effective regulatory and supervisory mechanism to protect the interests of the industry, the consumer and the environment. In the Eighth Plan, the "Special Tourism Areas" concept is being adopted, wherein a few tourist areas with high tourism potential will be identified and provided with full fledged infrastructure facilities. In 2002 ($10^{th}$ plan), Government of India had announced Tourism Policy. This policy gave the right to the central and state governments to individually, as well as collaboratively develop the Indian tourism sector. This policy also boosted the infusion of Foreign Direct Investment in the country.

**Challenges to the Tourism Sector:**

**1. Lack of Proper Infrastructure:**

Infrastructure needs for the travel and tourism range from physical infrastructure such as part of entry to modes of transport to urban infrastructure such as access roads, electricity, water supply, telecommunications, etc. The sector related to the travel and tourism industry includes airlines surface transports, accommodation and infrastructure and facilitation system. The poor infrastructure has been a major reason for the international tourist is skipping the country.

An entrenched framework of infrastructure which includes proper transportation facilities, health facilities, stable and uninterrupted connectivity and other human resources are mandatory for stable tourism. India was positioned 112$^{nd}$ in the ICT readiness component and was ranked 104$^{th}$ in the health and hygiene components of the WEF's Travel and Tourism Competitiveness Index, 2017. This basically mirrors the poor quality infrastructure our nation has. One of the significant reasons for this is the improper allocation of financial resources for the tourism sector. If we look at the 2017-18 budget, we can see that only ₹ 1840 crore was allocated for a prospering and promising sector like tourism.

**2. Access and Connectivity:**

To harness India's tourism potential, several efforts are being taken for opening new destinations and exploring niche segments. However, infrastructure facilities such as air, road connectivity and hospitality services at these destinations and the connecting cities are inadequate. This remains a major hurdle for the development of tourism.

**3. Taxation:**

High taxes on the entire industry including the airline facilities, hotels and tour operators are highly expensive. This is the one main reason why India loses to other less expensive countries when it comes to tourism. For instance, consider the price of air tickets. It varies in all the 29 states.

**4. Insufficient Promotion and Marketing:**

Great promotion and enough marketing push are excessively indispensable for a nation's travel industry improvement. Be that as it may, in India, the financial backing allotted to help and advance the travel industry is moderately less contrasted with other tourist destinations. At present, India needs a colossal move from the conventional marketing techniques that are still being followed to a much modern approach.

**5. Lack of Publicity:**

Lack of publicity for good tourist destinations among the travelers and also lack of good education to the locals on receiving guests and hosting them. Also, lack of publicity on cuisines and cultures.

6. **Amenities:**

Amenities at various tourist locations and en route need to be improved. These include basic amenities such as drinking water, well maintained and clean waiting rooms and toilets, first aid, etc.

7. **Human Resource:**

Availability of skilled manpower is a major challenge faced by the travel and tourism industry. To sustain growth in the travel and tourism industry, trained manpower or workforce is required. Highly skilled and potential men hold an inevitable part of the tourism sector. To maintain the growth of our Indian travel and tourism industry, a large number of skilled manpower is required at different levels. In the past years, there was an exploding increase in manpower for other sectors like banking, engineering and medicine. This gradually prompted abatement in the human resources available for the tourism sector. Thus at present, there is a huge demand for the workforce in both the hospitality and tourism sectors.

8. **Information and Communication:**

Though the official languages of the republic of India are standard Hindi and English yet the government of India has given 22 languages of the $8^{th}$ schedule the status of official languages. Because of such diversity in the regional languages, the foreign tourist has to face the problem of communication with the locals.

9. **Security and Safety:**

India is highly lacking on this attribute of competitiveness. The major reasons being the internal community riots and also the terrorist attacks faced from time to time. The country is highly unsafe for females and there is poor discipline as well as political instability in the country.

10. **Policies and Proper Implementation:**

Today, tourism has become more inclusive of new concepts which require the support of the government to develop and flourish. There is a need to propagate these concepts with dedicated policies formed for their development. Effective implementation of these policies will help in the growth of the industry overall. Few states like Kerala, Gujarat, Madhya Pradesh, Karnataka are taking pro-active measures in policy formation and implementation. Some of them have also drafted separate policies for specific segments like Eco-tourism. This has helped the states immensely to develop tourism infrastructure and increase their tourist arrivals. Such initiatives are required from other dormant states to create a uniform development of tourism infrastructure. Industry players need dynamic and far sighted policies by the government to help them boost tourism. Often, the major problem is that policies are formulated but are not clear and lack proper implementation. Policy-makers need to be more proactive in their approach to boost hospitality development in the country. There is a huge need for transparency in policy formation and clarity in their implementation. Government and industry need to work together to create strong hospitality and tourism development across the country.

**Prospects:**

India is gifted with massive diversity in culture, geography and art which pull in a colossal measure of voyagers to the nation. Different forms of tourism that are being introduced in recent years are also helping to build up the country's tourism industry. Medical tourism, eco-tourism, adventure tourism and cruise tourism have also gained a lot of popularity and attention among foreigners now and have the potential for high growth in the near future. The Himalayas are the greatest assets of India in adventure tourism. Tourism industry for India is a beautifully prospering and promising field. Taking sufficient measures to confront the difficulties presented and further enhancing the prospects can guarantee unlimited chances and development of the nation.

### 1.2.6 Banking Sector

The banking industry in India has a huge canvas of history which covers the traditional banking practices from the time of Britishers to the reforms period, nationalization to privatization of banks and now increasing numbers of foreign banks in India. Therefore, banking in India has been traversing through a long journey. Banking industry in India has also achieved new height with the changing times. The use of technology has brought a revolution in the working style of the banks. Nevertheless, the fundamental aspects of banking that is trust and confidence of the people on the institution remain the same. The majority of the banks are still successful in keeping with the confidence of the shareholders as also the stakeholders. However, with the changing dynamics banking business also brings new kind of risk exposure.

The Indian Banking system is unique in the banking history of any country in the world. It is very interesting to study the evolution of Indian Banking in terms of organization, functions, financial matter, socio-economic role, different problems and solutions. During the period of last five decades many macro-economic developments, monetary and banking policies, regulations and the external situation have taken place. Only due to this evolution of Indian banking occured in different ways.

**Banking and Economic Development:**

Banking system plays a vital role in the economic development of the country. In the process of economic development the contribution of banking system is mainly for capital formation, creation of money, strengthen the link between organized and unorganized sector, provision of long term loans, helping agricultural and small scale industry, entrepreneurial development, regulation of flow of national savings, maintaining balance of trade, catalyst in social change and effective implementation of monetary policy.

**Recent Banking Trends:**

The growing competition, growing expectations have led to increased awareness amongst banks on the role and importance of technology in banking. Banking today has transformed into a technology intensive and customer friendly model with a focus on convenience. Recent trends are as follows:

- **E-Cheques:** E-Cheques have replaced the conventional paper cheque. In India, Negotiable Instruments Act has already been amended to include truncated cheque and e-cheque instruments.
- **Real Time Gross Settlement (RTGS):** RTGS introduced in India since March, 2004 is a system through which electronic instructions can be given by banks to transfer funds from their account to the account of another bank.
- **Electronic Funds Transfer (EFT):** It is a system whereby anyone who wants to make payment to another person can approach his bank and make cash payment or give instructions to transfer funds directly from his own account to the bank account of the receiver.
- **Electronic Clearing Service (ECS):** It is a retail payment system that can be used to make bulk payment of a similar nature. It is meant for companies and government departments to make and receive large volumes of payment.
- **Automated Teller Machine (ATM):** It enables the customers to withdraw their money at any time without interacting with a human teller.
- **Point of Sale Terminal:** It is a computer terminal that is linked online to the computerized customer information files in a bank and

magnetically encoded plastic transaction card that identifies the customer to the computer. During transactions the customer's account is debited and the retailers account is credited by the computer for the amount of purchase.

- **Tele Banking:** It facilitates the customer to do entire non-cash related banking on telephone. Under this devise, Automatic Voice Recorder is used for smaller queries and transactions.

**Challenges to Indian Banking Sector:**

As banks develop their strategies for giving customers access to their accounts through various advanced services like e-banking, mobile banking and net banking, they should also regard this emerging platform as a potential catalyst for generating operational efficiencies and as a vehicle for new revenue sources. India's banking sector has made rapid strides in reforming and aligning itself to the new competitive business environment. The major challenges faced by banks are;

**1. Unhedged Forex Exposures:**

The wild gyrations in the forex market have the potential to inflict significant stress in the books of Indian companies who have heavily borrowed abroad. This stress, besides impacting repayment of forex liabilities, eventually hampers their debt repayment capability to the domestic lenders as well. It is precisely with this consideration that RBI has been advocating a curb on the increasing tendency of the corporates to dollarize their debts without adequate risk mitigation. Our supervision of banks' books has highlighted the need for the banks to have more robust policies for risk mitigation on account of unhedged foreign currency exposure of their corporate borrowers. Inadequacies of data further complicate the impact assessment of such exposures across the banking system. The banks have been advised to factor in this risk into their policies/pricing decision and also devise means for sharing of information on such exposures amongst themselves. Regulatory guidelines have also since been issued outlining the capital and provisioning requirements for exposure to entities with significant unhedged forex exposures.

**2. Human Resources Issues:**

The banks need to continuously enhance the skill levels of their employees so as to remain viable and competitive and to take advantage of new opportunities. The banking personnel, across the cadres need to be suitably trained to acquire necessary skill sets to perform their jobs more efficiently. The biggest challenge is to build capacity at a rate which matches the loss of existing talent and skills to retirement, poaching and resignations. The training initiatives must ensure that the available talent pool in the banks is able to always keep pace with the fast changing ways in which banking is conducted. Of course, in these challenges also lie an inherent opportunity for banks to redraw their organizational profile and to create HR systems and processes best suited to the needs of the future.

**3. High Transaction Costs:**

A major concern before the banking industry is the high transaction cost of carrying non-performing assets in their books. The growth has led to strains in the operational efficiency of banks and the accumulation of non-performing assets (NPA's) in their loan portfolios.

**4. Globalization of Regulation-Making Process:**

As it is alluded to a little earlier, banking regulations are getting increasingly globalized, subject of course to certain national discretions. As members of the standard setting bodies like BCBS and FSB, we are committed to implement these regulations in our jurisdictions. There is a process for peer review of regulatory guidelines issued by various jurisdictions to ascertain compliance with the global standards, failure to adhere to which would render the jurisdiction non-compliant to the standards. While we do participate in the regulation making process and suggest modifications to protect the rightful interests of the domestic economy, very often, we have to abide by the larger framework. One example viz. the large exposures regime, for which a consultation paper on new SBL/GBL norms has already been released by RBI.

**5. IT Revolution:**

The application of IT and e-banking is becoming the order of the day with the banking system heading towards virtual banking.

**6. Timely Technological up gradation:**

Already electronic transfers, clearings, settlements have reduced transaction times. To face competition, it is necessary for banks to absorb the technology and upgrade their services.

**7. Intense Competition:**

The RBI and Government of India kept banking industry open for the participants of private sector banks and foreign banks and these banks have spearheaded the hi-tech revolution.

**8. Privacy and Safety:**

Privacy of customer's information and safety of their savings is one of the topmost priority of bank. This goes a long way in influencing customer behavior in the choice of payment methods.

**9. Global Banking:**

The impact of globalization becomes a challenge for the domestic enterprises as they are bound to compete with global players. There are 36 foreign banks operating in India which have become a major challenge for Nationalized and Private Sector Banks.

**10. Financial Inclusion:**

Most of the Indian citizens don't use banking system for their financial requirements. It has become a necessity to create the awareness and importance of banks amongst people.

**11. Risk Management System:**

Banks need to have in place a fair and differentiated risk based pricing of products and services since capital comes at a cost. Banks put the risk management architecture in place to meet the regulatory requirements without using the risk inputs for taking business decisions. The risk is not properly priced for various products. The most challenging part is the availability, integrity and reliability of data.

Risk is inevitable in the banking business and hence, a sound risk management framework is the touchstone of an efficient bank. The risk management effectively aims at balancing the Risk-Return Trade-off which is "maximizing return for a given risk" and "minimizing risk for a given return". The responsibility of setting a risk appetite for the bank as a whole is that of the Board and the Top Management. In practice, however, we seldom see the articulation of an objective risk appetite statement by the PSBs. If you haven't set out a risk limit for each type of risk that the bank runs and an aggregate risk appetite for the bank as a whole, how do you measure and monitor risk? We must understand that risk management is integral to the success of the bank and hence, the Top Management should strive to put in place an efficient risk management framework keeping in view the changing market dynamics and the regulatory prescriptions.

**12. Human Resource Management:**

This is an area where most of our banks, especially the PSBs, are found lacking. In their eagerness to expand their core business they tend to forget the relevance of human expertise which drives their business in a sustainable manner. The complexities of modern banking and the dependence on IT makes it all the more important why the banks should have requisite manpower with right amount of knowledge and experience at appropriate places.

**13. Standardization and Capacity Build-up:**

While any development in offering electronic services is welcome, stand-alone systems not only work in silos but also fragment the market to some extent. Hence, as the payments eco-system matures, inter-operability becomes essential, for which standardization in processes and procedures is a pre-requisite. This not only facilitates uniformity in transaction handling but also enables uniform customer experiences.

**14. Partnerships with non-banks:**

It is imperative that banks also see the potential for synergetic growth by partnering with these non-banks and leveraging on their strengths so as to reap efficiency gains for both the entities. We have seen instances of such partnership, particularly with MNOs acting as BCs. Similar developments should occur in other areas too. A word of caution is, however, essential – banks cannot abdicate their responsibilities towards customers in ensuring safe and secure services, particularly in scenarios where a large part of the activities involved in payments are outsourced.

**15. Growth of Banking:**

The Indian banking industry experienced sustained productivity growth, which was driven mainly by technological progress. Foreign banks appear to have acted as technological innovators when competition increased which added to the competitive pressure in the market.

**16. Employees Retention:**

Long-time banking employees are becoming disenchanted with the industry and are often resistant to perform up to new expectations. The diminishing employee morale results in decreased revenue. Due to the intrinsically close ties between staff and clients, losing those employees completely can mean the loss of valuable customer relationships.

**17. Social and Ethical Aspects:**

Here are some banks, which proactively undertake the responsibility to bear the social and ethical aspects of banking. This is a challenge for commercial banks to consider these aspects in their working. Apart from profit maximization, commercial banks are supposed to support those organizations which have some social concerns.

**18. Rural Market:**

Banking in India is fairly mature in terms of supply, product range and reach, even though reach in rural India still remains a challenge for the private sector and foreign banks.

In terms of quality of assets and capital adequacy, Indian banks are considered to have clean, strong and transparent balance sheets relative to other banks in comparable economies in its region. For example recently, ICICI Bank Ltd. merged the Bank of Rajasthan Ltd. in order to increase its reach in rural market and market share significantly. Recently, SBI has merged State Bank of Indore in 2010.

**19. Enhancing Corporate Governance:**

Banks are special organizations because their managers have a fiduciary duty to depositors as well as shareholders and thus, a solution to the 'principal agent problem' aimed at maximizing shareholder value is inappropriate. Therefore, the good Corporate Governance of banks requires regulation to balance the interests of depositors and taxpayers with those of the shareholders. Moreover, banks are important participants in the payment and settlement system and as such corporate governance is highly relevant for them.

**20. Emerging Challenges:**

1. Deceleration in economic growth impacting expansion of banking sector.
2. Maintaining asset quality in the face of growing non-performing assets and restructuring of advances.
3. Augmenting capital and maintaining prudential capital.
4. Preserving and augmenting profitability in a stressed environment.
5. Implementing financial inclusion and Direct Benefits Transfer.
6. Increased competition from both within the banking sector with various banks becoming aggressive.
7. Adopting and adapting to technological changes/innovation to meet regulatory norms and tap alternative channels.
8. Improving quality of human resources for working efficiently under the latest technological developments.
9. Capital mobilization.
10. Implementation of Basel III.

## 1.3 RECENT TRENDS IN INDIAN SERVICE SECTOR

### 1.3.1 Digital Economy

A Digital India not only means empowerment for citizens but also offers significant scope for economic progress and growth and the opportunity to position India as a global technology hub and knowledge economy that other developing countries can learn from and emulate. In order to achieve this however, there needs to be a concerted effort to drive and follow through with effective change as well as a shift in mind-set from the traditional approach. What is really needed is the development of a larger innovation ecosystem in the country- one that fosters creativity, collaboration, partnerships and shared technical know-how to create disruptive business models, products and services that will fuel India's Digital transformation.

The Digital India initiative is a dream project of the Government to transform India into a digitally empowered society and knowledge economy. It is centered on three vision areas;

**1. Digital Infrastructure as a Utility to Every Citizen:**

The government is planning to provide high-speed internet connectivity to 250,000 Gram Panchayats which will be a core utility for digital inclusion. The citizens will be provided with a digital identity which will be unique, lifelong, online and valid. There will be easy access to Common Service Centers and a shareable private space for every citizen on a public cloud.

**2. Governance and Services on Demand:**

Under this vision, all the government departments will be seamlessly integrated with high-speed optical fiber, which will improve inter operability of these organizations and will result in real-time service delivery from online or mobile platform. Apart from this, the government is planning to make all citizen entitlements portable through cloud for easy and country-wide access and to digitally transform the services for improving ease of doing business in India. The government also plans to use the power of Geographic Information Systems (GIS) for decision support systems and development.

**3. Digital Empowerment of Citizens:**

This vision is to empower citizens through digital literacy and universal access to digital resources. e.g. all documents/certificates to be available on cloud and in Indian languages. Government also wants to provide collaborative digital platforms for participatory governance. e.g. MyGov website for crowd sourcing ideas.

These three vision areas further encompass nine themes or 'pillars' of Digital India, these are;

(i) Public Internet Access Programme.

(ii) Universal Access to Phones.

(iii) E-Governance: Reforming government through Technology.

(iv) Broadband Highways.
(v) Electronics Manufacturing Target net zero imports.
(vi) e_Kranti-Electronic delivery of services.
(vii) Early Harvest Programs.
(viii) Information for All.
(ix) IT for Jobs.

**Impacts of Digital India:**

The Digital India project provides a huge opportunity to use the latest technology to redefine the paradigms of service delivery. A digitally connected India can help in improving social and economic condition of people living in rural areas through development of non-agricultural economic activities apart from providing access to education, health and financial services. However, it is important to note that ICT alone cannot directly lead to overall development of the nation. The overall growth and development can be realized through supporting and enhancing elements such as literacy, basic infrastructure, overall business environment, regulatory environment, etc.

**Economic Impact:**

According to one study, the Digital India plan could boost GDP up to $1 trillion by 2025. It can play a key role in macro-economic factors such as GDP growth, employment generation, labor productivity, growth in number of businesses and revenue leakages for the Government. As per the World Bank report, a 10% increase in mobile and broadband penetration increases the per capita GDP by 0.81% and 1.38% respectively in the developing countries. India is the 2$^{nd}$ largest telecom market in the world with 915 million wireless subscribers and world's 3$^{rd}$ largest Internet market with almost 259 million broadband users. There is still a huge economic opportunity in India as the tele-density in rural India is only 4510 where more than 65% of the population lives. Future growth of telecommunication industry in terms of number of subscribers is expected to come from rural areas as urban areas are saturated with a tele-density of more than 160%.The digital platform can enable more creative and service-oriented business models that create employment opportunities. The Digital India project itself will create employment opportunities for 17 million people directly or indirectly which will help in fighting against unemployment problems in India. Government has planned to give IT training to 100 million students in smaller towns and villages as employment opportunity in IT sector is very high in India.

**Social Impact:**

Social sectors such as education, health-care and banking are unable to reach out to the citizens due to obstructions and limitations such as middlemen, illiteracy, ignorance, poverty, lack of funds, information and investments. These challenges have led to an imbalanced growth in the rural and urban areas with marked differences in the economic and social status of the people in these areas. Modern ICT makes it easier for people to obtain access to services and resources. The penetration of mobile devices may be highly useful as a complimentary channel to public service delivery apart from creation of entirely new services which may have an enormous impact on the quality of life of the users and lead to social modernization.

**Recent Trends:**

India is one of the largest and fastest-growing markets for digital consumers with 560 million internet subscribers in 2018. Indian mobile data users consume 8.3 gigabits (GB) of data each month on average, compared with 5.5 GB for mobile users in China and somewhere in the range of 8.0 to 8.5 GB in South Korea, an advanced digital economy. Indians have 1.2 billion mobile phone subscriptions and downloaded more than 12 billion apps in 2018. Our analysis of 17 mature and emerging economies reveals that India is digitizing faster than any other country.

The public and private sectors are both propelling digital consumption growth. The government has enrolled more than 1.2 billion Indians in its biometric digital identity programme, Aadhaar, and brought more than 10 million businesses onto a common digital platform through a goods and services tax. Competitive offerings by telecommunication firms have turbo charged internet subscriptions and data consumption, which quadrupled in both 2017 and 2018 and helped bridge a digital divide; India's lower-income states are growing faster than higher-income ones in internet infrastructure and subscriptions. Based on current trends, we estimate that India will increase the number of internet users by about 40 percent to between 750 million and 800 million and double the number of smartphones to between 650 million and 700 million by 2023.

Digital applications could proliferate across most sectors of India's economy. By 2025, core digital sectors such as IT and business process management, digital communication services and electronics manufacturing could double their GDP level to \$355 billion to \$435 billion. Newly digitising sectors, including agriculture, education, energy, financial services, health-care, logistics, and retail, as well as government services and labour markets, could each create \$10 billion to \$150 billion of incremental economic value in 2025 as digital applications in these sectors help raise output, save costs and time, reduce fraud and improve matching of demand and supply.

According to one estimates, the productivity unlocked by the digital economy could create 60 million to 65 million jobs by 2025, many of them requiring functional digital skills. Retraining and redeployment will be essential to help 40 to 45 million workers whose jobs could be displaced or transformed.

New digital ecosystems are already visible, reshaping consumer-producer interactions in agriculture, health-care, retail, logistics and other sectors. Opportunities span over such areas as data-driven lending and insurance payouts in the farm sector to digital solutions that map out the most efficient routes and monitor cargo movements on India's highways. In health-care, patients could turn to tele-consultations via digital voice or HD video, and in retail, brick-and-mortar stores would find value from being part of e-commerce platforms.

All stakeholders will need to respond effectively if India is to achieve its digital potential. Executives will need to anticipate the digital forces that will disrupt their businesses and invest in building capabilities, including partnering with universities and outsourcing or acquiring talent to deliver digital projects. Governments will need to invest in digital infrastructure and public data that organisations can leverage even as they put in place strong privacy and security safeguards. Capturing the gains of the digital economy will require more ease in creating, scaling and exiting startups as well as policies to facilitate retraining and new-economy jobs for workers. Individuals will need to update themselves about how the digital economy could affect them as workers and consumers and prepare to capture its opportunities.

**Pioneering Digital with 5G:**

5G is expected to support many applications/use cases in India and play a larger role in the socio-economic uplift of the country. India specific applications need to be developed with the coordinated efforts of industry, academia and start-up community. It is very important to initiate field trials of 5G and test specific use cases. All stakeholders must utilize the time between now and 2020 to fine-tune 5G use cases and help build the ecosystem. 5G is set to transform the country by offering more jobs, increase GDP and support new and cutting edge technologies such as artificial intelligence and robotics. 5G will be a major catalyst for Digital India.

**India has the Potential to Create Considerable Economic Value by 2025:**

$ 130 billion to $ 170 billion in financial services (including digital payments); $ 50 billion to $ 65 billion in agriculture; $ 25 billion to $35 billion in retail and e-commerce (including supply chain); $ 25 billion to $ 30 billion in logistics and transportation; and roughly $ 10 billion in areas such as energy and health-care. Greater digitisation of government services and benefits transfers could yield economic value of $ 20 billion to $ 40 billion combined and up to $ 70 billion from more efficient skill training and job market matching using digital platforms by 2025.

**The Impending Challenges:**

The Digital India initiative is an ambitious project of the Government and is, by far, the biggest ever conceived. There are many challenges discussed below that could come in the way of successful completion of the project.

**(1) High Cost of Implementation:** Approximate cost of implementing this mammoth project is ₹ 1.13 trillion (including ongoing and new schemes).

**(2) Time Overrun:** The National Optic Fibre Network (NOFN) project which is the back-bone of the Digital India project has been delayed several times and is suffering two years' time overrun. The delayed project may lead to delay in other dependent projects and meeting the budget limit will be difficult.

**(3) Lack of Coordination Among Departments:** It is an umbrella project involving participation of several departments and demanding commitment and effort. Hence, strong leadership and timely support of all the involved entities will play a critical role.

**(4) Poor Private Participation:** To achieve timely completion of the projects extensive private participation is necessary. The private participation in the government projects in India is poor because of long and complex regulatory processes.

**(5) Uniform and Fast Adoption of Internet:** About 4 billion people in the world do not have internet connection and India comprises of 25% of them. India is the 4$^{th}$ largest smartphone market with almost 111 million smartphone users. Average monthly cost of 500MB mobile data plan on prepaid is \$ 3.4 in India against \$ 35.8 in Brazil, \$ 15.5 in China and \$17 in Russia. Despite lowest data tariffs in the world, adoption of internet in India is not encouraging. Faster adoption of Internet will be difficult due to illiteracy, affordability and availability of mobile devices and data tariffs, lack of local language content, lack of regionally relevant apps. Still the use of internet is low because of high data tariffs.

**(6) Infrastructure:** Though the National Optic Fibre Network (NOFN) project is aiming to build a nationwide high speed broadband by the end of the year 2016-17, there are other supporting infrastructure deficits, such as lack of robust and large data centers to hold the data of entire country. In addition, the last mile connectivity and the physical infrastructure at customer premises are unaffordable by most of the rural Indians. Infrastructure fulfillment is necessary with the NOFN project.

**(7) Cyber Security:** Nation Crime Records Bureau (NCRB) report shows the rapid increase in cybercrime in India by 50% from 2012 to 2013. There have been several incidences of cybercrime on corporate and individual level in the past few years. Putting the data of 1.2 billion people on the cloud could be risky and could threaten the security of individuals and the nation. Hence, the Digital India project demands very strong network security at all levels of operation.

## 1.3.2 E-Commerce

### E-commerce Industry in India:

Electronic commerce is presently an indispensable ingredient of India's trade facilitation policy. Since 1991, after economic reforms explicitly took place in India as a result of opening of the economy with a view to integrate itself with the global economy, the need to facilitate international trade both through policy and procedure reforms has become the foundation stone of India's trade and fiscal policies. As a result, last few years have witnessed a technological revolution accompanied by the wide-spread use of the internet, web technologies and their applications. Electronic commerce (e-commerce) as part of the information technology revolution became widely used in the world trade in general and Indian economy in particular. As a symbol of globalization, e-commerce represents the cutting edge of success in this digital age and it has changed and is still changing the way business is conducted around the world. The commercialization of the internet has driven electronic commerce to become one of the most capable channels for inter-organizational business processes. Consequently, internet growth has led to a host of new developments, such as decreased margins for companies as consumers turn more and more to the internet to buy goods and demand the best prices.

Although business-to-business transactions play an important part in e-commerce market, a share of e-commerce revenues in rapidly developing countries like India is generated from business to consumer transactions. E-commerce provides multiple benefits to the consumers in the form of availability of goods at lower cost, wider choice and saves time. People can buy goods with a click of mouse button without moving out of their house or office. Similarly, online services such as banking, ticketing (including airlines, bus, railways), bill payments, hotel booking, etc. have been of tremendous benefit for the customers. Online businesses like financial services, travel, entertainment, and groceries are all likely to grow. E-commerce evolved in various means of relationships within the business processes. It can be in the form of electronic advertising, electronic payment system, electronic marketing, electronic customer support service and electronic order and delivery.

E-commerce stands for electronic commerce and pertains to trading in goods and services through the electronic medium i.e. the internet or phone. On the internet, it pertains to a website, which sells products or services directly from the site using a shopping cart or shopping basket system and allows credit card payments. It involves conducting business with the help of the electronic media, making use of the information technology such as Electronic Data Interchange (EDI). In general connotation, e-commerce involves paperless transactions and usage of EDI (Electronic Data Interchange), electronic mail, bulletin boards, fax transmissions and electronic fund transfers. It refers to the process of trading goods and services through an electronic medium such as the internet.

The e-commerce business in India has seen exponential growth over the last decade. This growth is due to many contributory factors, including rapid adoption of technology by Indian consumers, large increases in the number of internet users, new enabling technologies, innovative business models and alternative payment options offered by e-commerce companies. Moreover, the high growth in e-commerce continues unabated, with the sector expecting to witness a steep increase in revenues in the coming years. The e-commerce industry was worth ₹ 351 (5.4 billion US $) billion in 2011, it grew at a CAGR of 37% to touch ₹ 1257 billion in 2015 and is estimated to become a ₹ 2,110 billion (31 billion US $) industry by 2016.

**Definitions of E-commerce:**

"E-commerce is understood to mean the production, distribution, marketing, sale or delivery of goods and services by electronic means". "E-commerce means buying and selling of goods and services including digital products over digital and electronic networks".

**The Asia Pacific Economic Co-operation ("APEC")**, "All business activity conducted using a combination of electronic communications and information processing technology".

**The United Nations Economic and Social Commission for Asia and the Pacific ("UNESCAP")**, "The process of using electronic methods and procedures to conduct all forms of business activity".

**Share of E-commerce in GDP:**

The Indian economy grew by 7% in October-December 2016 and is expected to grow at 7.1% in 2016-17. The e-commerce industry which was worth ₹ 1257 billion in 2015 is estimated to be contributing about 1% of GDP.

Segment-wise estimates for the share in GDP are also put out by some agencies. The B2CE-commerce segment accounted for 0.16% of India's GDP in 2013 and is estimated to be around 0.20% of GDP in 2016 (Statista.com).

**Table 1.9: Growth of e-commerce in India**

| Year | Total E-Commerce Transactions (in Million $) |
|---|---|
| 1998-99 | 31.38 |
| 1999-00 | 103.84 |
| 2007-08 | 1750.00 |
| 2008-09 | 3015.00 |
| 2009-10 | 4230.00 |
| 2010-11 | 6790.00 |
| 2011-12* | 10000.00 |

**Source:** Computer Engineering and Intelligent Systems, By Sarbapriya Ray, www.iiste.org, Vol 2, No.5, 2011* Projections.

**Government and Private Organizations and Industry Sectors Involvement in Ecommerce:**

**(a) Government Organizations:**

E-Portals or websites are promoted by the Government of India for e-commerce and compulsory online reservation, applications, payments, auctions, public-procurement, etc. A few examples of such portals are:

**1. https://www.ebiz.gov.in**

**India's Government to Business E-portal:**

Portal for central services like industrial license, company affairs, PAN1 and other CBDT (Central Board of Direct Taxes) related services, importer-exporter code and state services like application of several industrial and other business establishment NOCs2, MSME3 registration, allotment of scarce raw-materials like coal.

**2. www.gem.gov.in**

**Procurement of Goods by Government:**

Government e-Marketplace for public procurement of products and services by State and Central Governments and State and Central Public Sector Undertakings, etc.

**3. https://www.irctc.co.in**

**Train and Air Tickets booking:**

Online platform for reservation of tickets for Indian Railways and Airlines.

**4. http://www.mca.gov.in**

**Ministry of Corporate Affairs (MCA) for companies:**

The online MCA platform is the nodal e-platform for incorporation and other compliances for ROC (Registrar of Companies) registered companies and firms. This website is the gateway to services, guidance and other corporate affairs related information.

**5. https://eauction.gov.in**

**Auction by Government:**

Nodal e-auction platform used by the state and central governments of India, state and central public sector undertakings.

**6. https://onlineservices.tin.egov-nsdl.com/etaxnew/tdsnontds.jsp**

**Payment of Income Tax:**

For online payment of 'Tax Deducted at Source'.

**(b) Private Sector Organizations**

**Amazon:**

Marketplace for e-commerce B2C.

US-based Amazon provides small businesses including small stores, pharmacies, mobile retailers, small offices, nursing homes and restaurants a convenient online shopping experience that saves their time and money.

**Shopmatic:**

Technology company for removing the complexities of setting up an e-commerce business Singapore based Technology Company Shopmatic works by removing the complexities of setting up an e-commerce business.

**KartRocket:**

E-commerce software platform Kart Rocket empowers SMEs, small retailers and entrepreneurs to start their own online businesses.

**Bizongo:**

It helps by simplifying the sourcing and easy searching of right products.

**Industry buying:**

A platform for industrial goods and supplies, maintains fully catalogued collection of over 1.5 lakh units from brands across global geographies where regular buyers are offered credit and the purchasing process is quite straightforward.

**Tolexo:**

A platform for the SMEs, Tolexo provides consumer shopping experience for the largest collection of products needed by businesses, factories, offices and laboratories.

**Snapdeal:**

Founded in February 2010, Snapdeal.com is an online marketplace which claims to have an assortment of 15 million plus products across 500 plus categories from regional, national and international brands and retailers. Snapdeal has partnered with investors and individuals such as Soft Bank, Black Rock, Temasek, eBay Inc., Premji Invest, Intel Capital, Bessemer Venture Partners and Ratan Tata, among others.

**Flipkart:**

This is another market where one can purchase many books which are of all types and world famous authors books.

**Government Flagship Initiatives for Development of E-commerce:**

Government has undertaken several initiatives to boost the e-commerce sector in India. It has been leveraging e-commerce digital platforms to organize traditionally offline markets, even for agricultural produce. Amongst others, it has launched an e-market platform to connect farmers with mandies of various states to sell agro-commodities online. The government's flagship initiatives such as Digital India, Start-up India, Make in India and Skill India also contribute to the growth of e-commerce industry.

In March 2017, the government permitted 100% Foreign Direct Investment (FDI) in online retail of goods and services under the 'marketplace model' to legitimize existing businesses of the e-commerce companies in India and to attract more foreign investments in the sector. A market place model is an information technology platform run by an e-commerce entity on a digital and electronic network to act as a facilitator between buyers and sellers. 100% FDI is also allowed in B2B e-commerce in India. However, FDI is not permitted in the inventory based model of e-commerce, which is applicable to companies that own inventories of goods and services and sell directly to consumers using online platforms. Other major flagship initiatives of the Government are:-

**(i) Digital India:** One of the highly ambitious and biggest ever conceived projects is 'Digital India' which focuses on transforming India in to a digitally empowered and knowledge economy. The three key areas that have been identified to build digital infrastructure are core utility, enable government citizen services on demand and digital empowerment of citizens.

**(ii) Start-up India:** This program intends to build a strong eco-system for nurturing "innovation" and "exponential start-ups". The government of India has taken steps such as providing funding support through a "Fund of Funds" (with a corpus of INR 100 billion); (1.5 billion US $) 'Start-up India hub', a single point contact for the start-up ecosystem, tax exemptions for the initial three years and faster exit for start-ups.

**(iii) Make in India:** Aimed at India's industrial development, the key steps taken by the government of India are improving the business environment and enabling manufacturing and allowing FDI in key sectors. Key pillars of this program are 'research and innovation' and 'conducive business environment'.

**(iv) Skill India:** To bridge the shortage of skilled manpower, the government of India has set a target to train 400 million people under the new 'National Policy for Skill Development' by 2022.

**Major Contributory Factors to the Growth of E-commerce Industry in India:**

**(a) Faster Adoption of New Technology:**

Faster adoption of new technologies like the internet and smartphones has been one of the biggest drivers of e-commerce in India. About 402 million people in India are presently using the Internet. The number is further expected to reach 500 million users by 2017. It is estimated that by June 2016, the number of mobile internet users in India was 371 million.

**(b) India Fastest Growing Economy:**

India is amongst the fastest growing economies globally and higher income levels have made India one of the fastest-growing consumer markets in the world. Rising disposable income, changes in lifestyle and shopping patterns are some of the factors that have proved instrumental in driving the e-commerce industry in India.

**(c) Innovating Easy-to-Use Technologies:**

The e-commerce companies in India have been focusing on developing new applications suitable for mobiles/smart phones, enabling users to make online transactions through their devices with ease. Mobile applications have also assisted companies to enhance their geographical outreach and increase their communication level with the end-users through exchange of regular service updates and messages.

In addition, digital advertisements have also enabled e-commerce players to reach out to a wider audience/customers. Similarly, adoption of Search Engine Optimization (SEO) as an internet marketing strategy has also helped e-commerce companies improve their search engine rankings.

**(d) Choice of Payment Options:**

While e-commerce companies in India offer various payment options, most of the players have been offering 'cash-on-delivery' option to customers, despite incurring higher administration costs on account of such transactions as this is the most preferred mode of payment among consumers. Digital payment products and electronic wallets have also been launched to ease the payment process in e-commerce transactions.

**Challenges in the E-commerce Sector in India:**

E-commerce sectors have been facing multiple challenges in their business operations like taxation issues, incidents of fraud and issues with cyber security, intense competition and preference for payment in cash (COD) by customers, inadequate infrastructure and low digital literacy. There is no uniform tax structure across various states and there is ambiguity with respect to categorization of offerings into 'goods' or 'services'. Guidelines on taxation of certain transactions like e-wallets, cash on delivery, gift vouchers, etc. are not clearly defined. Some of these challenges are expected to be resolved after the implementation of the Goods and Services Tax (GST).

Incidents of distribution of counterfeit goods through e-commerce platform have also been increasing which has added to the woes of both consumers as well as e-commerce companies. This is mainly because of the absence of a trustworthy mechanism which can allow consumers to authenticate sellers or their products. Data/cyber security is another major challenge faced by the players as they deal with huge volumes of customer information, a lot of which is shared with third parties such as logistics providers raising concerns about exploitation by external entities.

Another challenge is payment by customers in cash. Receiving payment in cash (COD) makes the process laborious, risky and more expensive for the companies as their working capital requirement increases. Higher return ratio for goods sold online is also proving expensive and presenting challenges for companies. Incidentally, return percentage of orders in COD is much higher compared to online payments.

The e-commerce industry in India has seen intensified competition in the sector, which in turn has forced companies to adopt aggressive pricing policies, offering heavy discounts to customers and high commissions to vendors and other parties. This has exerted a lot of pressure on the profitability of the companies.

**Counterfeit Products:**

The e-commerce platforms are proved to be used for distribution of banned and counterfeit goods. This can happen when certain suppliers/distributors introduce counterfeit products in the supply chain alongside genuine products, making it difficult for e-commerce companies to detect counterfeits. Further, since the onus of ensuring product quality, authenticity and packaging rests on the sellers, the e-commerce companies, which act primarily as aggregators, are often unable to proactively detect counterfeits or inferior/faulty products that may be sold to customers via their networks.

**Due Diligence Checks Issues:**

While some of the leading e-commerce marketplaces have already established protocols to know their customers to help identify unscrupulous sellers, at times, the information obtained from sellers as part of these procedures can be misleading. For instance, while PAN numbers may be sought from sellers, there is no process to ensure that duplicate PAN numbers are not in use. Also, information pertaining to credentials of the seller such as market reputation, physical verification of the seller's premises, track record in ensuring product quality, litigation history, relationship check indicating conflict of interest and political interests is not available fully, which can jeopardize the business process.

**Government's Measures for Developing E-Commerce:**

**Introduction of Dedicated E-commerce Laws:**

India does not have a dedicated 'Data Protection and Privacy Law'. These requirements are partially being addressed from the application of provisions of other general laws in the country. It is therefore necessary that dedicated laws for the growth of e-commerce are promulgated including the laws for cyber security, Data protection and Privacy laws to give a boost to the growth of e-commerce in the country and to avoid unnecessary litigations.

**(a) Increase in Internet Penetration:**

At the heart of the e-commerce lies the ability to not just stay connected online but also to do so at a fast speed. India ranks relatively lower when compared with it's Asian counterparts, the U.S. and China in respect of availability of Internet speed. Additionally, many parts of rural India are yet to receive broadband connection. While efforts have been made in this direction, the Government plans to facilitate internet connectivity for over two lac Gram Panchayats. Public Private Partnership (PPP) projects in this area should be implemented for enhancing the reach of internet to rural parts of India.

**(b) Seamless Integration Between Government Departments and Agencies:**

An integrated and coordinated approach is needed between different government agencies such as policy-makers, Income Tax, Sales Tax, VAT, Excise and Registrar of Companies to ensure faster turnaround, efficiency and transparency for all stakeholders in the e-commerce ecosystem. With instances where one state is levying a flat entry tax on all e-commerce consignments and the other state imposing restrictive trade practices on e-commerce companies, it gives wrong messages. The government should ensure a uniform regulatory and tax structure across the states to prevent such instances from dampening the growth of e-commerce in India.

**(c) Faster Implementation of Initiatives:**

The government has already launched several initiatives such as Digital India, Skill India, Make in India and Start-up India. Faster implementation of these initiatives would have a positive impact on the route of e-commerce industry.

**(d) Regular Consultations with Stakeholders:**

A consultative approach with periodic interactions with all stakeholders, trade bodies and industry associations will help in building a uniform and favorable e-commerce ecosystem. There is a need to reach consensus on a domestic e-commerce policy like location of servers to effectively respond to a proposal of multilateral discipline in e-commerce. Under Information Technology Agreement (ITA-1), India has agreed to abolish tariffs on hardware, which went against its domestic electronics manufacturing industry. "If large chunk of future business is going to happen through e-commerce, giving up the right to impose tariffs in future may go against India's domestic players and eliminate a source of revenue. So, the country should reconsider this stand while negotiating on e-commerce in the international forums.

**(e) Accreditation and Rating of e-commerce Entities:**

There are a large number of heterogeneous e-commerce entities operating at various levels with non-uniform systems hindering possibilities of sustainable cross-border trade. Therefore, in the interest of bringing credibility to such e-commerce entities, a mechanism to provide accreditation and/or rating should be developed or facilitated by the government. This shall encourage confidence building among users by bringing in standardization of procedures, quality in service delivery and overall homogeneity in expectations across buyers and sellers in the country.

In order to achieve the desired standardization for the above said objectives, a designated facilitating and hand holding agency needs to be created in the country which should create online-systems with proper forward and backward linkages to enable the adherence of a standard model code for e-commerce.

### 1.3.3 E-Finance in India

Finance is a commercial term which refers to the use of monetary resource by an entrepreneur, firm or any business house in a project or venture. The state of a business in e-valuated by the position of its finance. E-finance as a provisioning financing instruments to business organization using electronic tools and technology for the length wise process and this incorporates the use of electronics channels for mobilizing e-finance services and electronic methods to set up proper finance conditions and deal with risk related to the finance itself. E-finance in simple words is use of internet and technologies in financial services. It has enabled the people to have any financial transactions without any human interaction. It saves times, reduces the paper work and chances of fraud. Nowadays with the emergence of e-commerce, e-finance has become a buzz word among the entrepreneurs, business firms and investors. Due to the encouraging awareness about the use of internet and computer technology in commercial purpose, e-finance has emerged as solution to simplify the complexions involved in dealing with finance. It is somewhat shift of system of financial services from the real world to virtual one.

E-finance includes e-banking, e-payment, e-trading, e-cash, digital currency and International Mobile Phone Services (IMPS). These major factors are impacting financial services, advances in information technology, massive cost reductions in technology and communications cost. In the Business to Customer (B2C) category are include e-shops, shopping malls, e-broking, e-auction, e-banking, service providers like travel related services, financial services, etc. education, entertainment and any other form of business targeted at the final consumer.

**Definition of E-Finance:**

E-finance is defined as the, "Provision of financial services and markets using electronic communication and competition".

"All which relates to the linking of business, finance and banking via electronic means, encompassing information gathering, processing, retrieval and transmission of data as well as the transmission, purchase and selling of goods and services".

Through e-finance has evolved a new field retail finance and is still in budding stage. It has a greater importance and is playing a vital role for developing economies likes India, China and Brazil. The proposed e-finance portal provides an integrated enterprise platform for retail banking services as well as for other financial services.

**Scope of E-Finance:**

**Financial Market:** Financial market refers to the market where financial assets are exchanged by dealers such as stock exchange market. By e-finance facility, it has become easier to perform the activities related to financial market through internet technology.

**Online Banking:** Online banking began in mid 1990s and is also called as e-banking. It refers to the process of getting connected to the official website of the bank through the internet and performing the task even if the costumer is not present in the bank. It enables the user to maintain his financial activities through the e-banking system.

**Internet Transaction:** Generally, it includes e-cash, e-payment, digital currency and ATM. It is a way to transact through the internet without using real currency.

**Online Trade Finance:** Trade finance provides services that resolve payment and delivery issues between buyers and sellers in international trade.

**Credit Information and Management:** E-finance becomes the most powerful tool to gather data of various departments and markets. Many research companies like CRISIL are providing useful data.

**Present Scenario:**

By the end of 1990s, e-finance technology and argued affected all aspects of the business of banking and financial intermediation, with the possible exception of lending to large business. The internet has evolved from a mere information dispensing vehicle into a robust transaction facilitating environment. New software tools and safer architecture with multiple security and access control structures have enabled banks to take advantage of internet technology and software protocols for devising a host of products and services which could be distributed and made available through internet. E-finance encompasses all financial products and services which are available to customer through the internet.

**Table 1.10: Number of Banks Having Websites and Internet Banking**

| Bank | Number of Banks | Number of Banks with website | Number of Internet Banks | Internet Banks as % |
|---|---|---|---|---|
| Private Sector | 28 | 28 | 17 | 100 |
| Public Sector Total | 28 | 20 | 18 | 90 |
| SBI | 8 | - | - | - |
| Nationalized | 20 | 20 | 18 | 90 |
| Foreign Banks | 29 | 29 | 6 | 20.7 |
| All Banks | 85 | 84 | 49 | 57.6 |

**Source:** International Journal of Research (ijr) Vol-1 issue, 4 May 2014.

ICICI was the first bank to launch the website for banking in 1996. Later on, in 1997 ICICI primarily started the internet banking and also online bill payment started in 1999. In India, it is governed by Information Technology Act, by 2000, internet banking, guidelines of the central bank and India is the 2nd country in Asia to initiate technology related act. Now about 28 percent of brokerage services are provided online in industrial countries and markets. In following table, data of some banks having website and internet banking (in 1919 government merged some banks. Hence, now 12 banks are nationalized is shown banks).

## POINTS TO REMEMBER

- The service sector includes all activities which people offer, their knowledge and time to improve productivity, performance and sustainability.
- In recent past, the service sector has been working as booster or major force for the other two sectors of economy viz. industry and agriculture.
- In 2018-19, service sector's contributes 54.3% to GDP of the country.
- The recent trends in Indian Service Sector includes, emergence of digital economy, growth of E-commerce and E-finance.
- India has a strong potential to develop a strong competitive advantage in knowledge based industries like software industry.
- Tourism industry is one of the largest segments under the service sector of the Indian economy.

## QUESTIONS FOR DISCUSSION

1. Explain the role of service sector in Indian economy.
2. Explain the growth of service sector in Indian economy.
3. Narrate the current scenario of insurance sector in Indian economy.
4. State the challenges to health sector of the Indian economy.
5. Explain the recent banking trends.
6. Explain the challenges to the tourism sector in India.
7. Explain the challenges to Indian banking sector.
8. Write short notes on :
   (A) Education sector (B) Digital Economy
   (C) E-commerce (D) E-finance

***

Unit **2**...

# Banking Environment

***Contents ...***



## 2.1 BANKING - DEFINITION, FUNCTIONS, CHANGING STRUCTURE OF BANKING IN INDIA - NEW PRIVATE BANKS, SMALL BANKS, PAYMENT BANKS

### Origin and Evolution of the Word Bank:

According to some authors the word "Bank" itself is derived from the word *"Bancus"* or *"Banque"* that is a bench. The early bankers, the Jews in Lombardy, transacted their business on benches in the market place, When, a banker failed, his 'Banco' was broken up by the people; it was called 'Bankrupt' This etymology is however, ridiculed by Mcleod on the ground that "The Italian Money changers as such were never called Banchier in the middle ages." It is generally said that the word "Bank" has been originated in Italy. In the middle of the 12$^{th}$ century, there was a great financial crisis in Italy due to war. To meet the war expenses, the government of that period forced a subscribed loan on citizens of the country at the interest of 5% per annum. Such loans were known as 'Compare', 'minto', etc. The most common name was "*Monte*'. In Germany the word 'Monte was named as '*Bank*' or '*Banke*'. According to some writers, the word 'Bank' has been derived from the word bank. It is also said that the word 'bank' has been derived from the word '*Banco*' which means a bench. It is interesting to trace the origin of the word 'bank' in the modern sense, to the German word *"Banck"* which means, heap or mound or joint stock fund. From this, the Italian word *'Banco'*, meaning heap of money was coined. Some people have the opinion that the word "bank" is derived from the French words *"bancus"* or *"banque"* which means a 'bench'. If a banker failed, his 'banque' (bench) was broken up by the people; hence the word "bankrupt" has come. In simple term, bankrupt means a person who has lost all his money, wealth or financial resources. Whatever be the origin of the word, 'Bank' as Professor Ram Chandra Rao says, "It would trace the history of banking in Europe from the Middle Ages.

Today, the word bank is used as a comprehensive term for a number of institutions carrying on certain kinds of financial business. In practice, the word 'Bank' means which borrows money from one class of people and again lends money to another class of people for interest or profit.

Actually, meaning of bank is not specified in any regulation or act. In India, different people have different types of meanings for bank. Normal salary earner knows that it is a saving institution, current account holder or businessman knows bank as a financial institutions and many other. Bank is not for profit making, it creates saving activity for salary earner. Thus, the origin of the word bank can be traced as Banck - German (Joint stock fund), Banco - Italian (Heap of money), Bancus / Banque - French (Bench/ chest a place where valuables are kept), Bank - English (common meaning prevalent today, i.e., as an institution accepting money as deposit for lending) Banking as accepting for the purpose of lending or investment of deposits of money from the public, repayable on demand or otherwise and withdrawable by cheque, draft, order or otherwise. Any institution other than a banking company to accept deposit money from public withdrawal by cheque. In other words, the combination of the functions of acceptance of public and deposits and withdrawal of the money by cheques by an institution cannot be performed without the approval of Reserve Bank.

### 2.1.1 Definitions of Bank

**Indian Banking Regulation Act, 1949 Section 5 (1) (b) of the Banking Regulation Act 1949 :** Banking has defined as, *"Accepting for the purpose of the lending of investment of deposits of money from public repayable on demand or otherwise and withdrawable by cheques, draft, order or otherwise."*

**Oxford Dictionary** defines bank as *"Bank is an establishment for custody of money received from or on behalf of its customers. It's essential duty is to pay their drafts unit. It's profits arise from the use of the money left employed them."*

**Crowther** defines a bank as, *"One that collects money from those who have it to spare or who are saving it out of their income and lends the money so collected to those who require it".*

**Dr. L. Hart** says that the bankers are *"One who in the ordinary course of business honors cheques drawn upon him by persons from and for whom he receives money on current accounts"*.

**Sir Kinley**, *"A bank is an establishment which makes to individuals such advances money as may be required and to which individuals entrust money when not required by them for use"*.

**Background of Banking in India:**

The East India Company laid the foundation for modern banking in the first-half of the 19th century with the establishment of the three banks:

- Bank of Bengal in 1809
- Bank of Bombay in 1840
- Bank of Madras in 1843

These banks were also known as "Presidency Banks" and they functioned well as independent units. In 1920, the all presidency banks were amalgamated to form the Imperial Bank of India which was run by European Shareholders. On the basis of the recommendation of the Banking Enquiry Committee, the Reserve Bank of India Act was passed in 1934. Accordingly, the Reserve Bank of India was established in 1935. In 1955, the Imperial Bank of India was nationalized and was given the name "State Bank of India", to act as the principal agent of RBI and to handle banking transactions all over the country. It was established under State Bank of India Act, 1955. In the 1960s, the Indian banking industry had become an important tool to facilitate the development of the Indian economy. The nationalization took place in the country in 1969. Fourteen major Indian commercial banks were nationalized and also in 1980 six more banks were nationalized. Recently, government of India announced that eight national banks will be merged in other twelve banks. Hence 12 banks will be functioning as national banks in India.

In the year 1991 under the chairmanship of M. Narasimham, a committee was set up which worked for the liberalization of banking practices. In this year were introduced many more products and facilities in the banking sector in its reforms measures. The banking industry has undergone rapid changes, followed by a series of fundamental developments. Most significant among them is the advancement in information technology as well as communication system. This has changed technology as well as communication system. This has changed the very concept of traditional banking activities and has been instrumental behind broadening the dissemination of financial information along with lowering the costs of many financial activities. Information Technology and the Communication Networking Systems have revolutionized the functioning of the banks.

### 2.1.2 The Functions of Bank

**A. Primary Functions:**

**1. Receiving Deposits:**

The first and foremost function of commercial bank is to receive or collect deposits from the public in different forms of accounts e.g. current, savings, term deposits. No interest is charged in the current account, lower rate of interest is charged in the savings account and comparatively higher interest rates charged in fixed deposits. Thus, commercial bank builds up customer network.

**1. Time Deposits:**

These are deposits repayable after a certain fixed period. These deposits are not withdrawable by cheque, draft or by other means. It includes the following.

**(a) Fixed Deposits:** The deposits can be withdrawn only after expiry of certain period say 3 years, 5 years or 10 years. The banker allows a higher rate of interest depending upon the amount and period of time. Previously, the rates of interest payable on fixed deposits were determined by the Reserve Bank.

Presently banks are permitted to offer interest as determined by each bank. However, banks are not permitted to offer different interest rates to different customers for deposits of same maturity period, except in the case of deposits of ₹ 15 lakhs and above. These days the banks accept deposits even for 15 days or one month, etc. In times of urgent need for money, the bank allows premature closure of fixed deposits by paying interest at reduced rate. Depositors can also avail of loans against Fixed Deposits. The Fixed Deposit Receipts cannot be transferred to other persons.

**(b) Recurring Deposits:** In recurring deposit, the customer opens an account and deposits a certain sum of money every month. After a certain period, say 1 year or 3 years or 5 years, the accumulated amount along with interest is paid to the customer. It is very helpful to the middle and poor sections of the people. The interest paid on such deposits is generally on cumulative basis. This deposit system is a useful mechanism for regular savers of money.

**(c) Cash Certificates:** Cash certificates are issued to the public for a longer period of time. It attracts the people because its maturity value is in multiples of the sum invested. It is an attractive and high yielding investment for those who can keep the funds for a longtime. It is a very useful account for meeting future financial requirements at the occasion of marriage, education of children, etc. Cash certificates are generally issued at a discount to face value. It means a cash certificate of ₹ 1,00,000 payable after 10 years can be purchased now, say for ₹ 20,000.

**2. Demand Deposits:**

These are the deposits which may be withdrawn by the depositor at any time without previous notice. It is withdrawable by cheque/draft. It includes the following:

**(a) Savings Deposits:** The savings deposit promotes thrift among people. The savings deposits can only be held by individuals and non-profit institutions. The rate of interest paid on savings deposits is lower than that of time deposits. The savings account holder gets the advantage of small income in the form of interests. But, there are some restrictions on withdrawals. Corporate bodies and business firms are not allowed to open SB Accounts. Presently, interest on SB Accounts is determined by RBI. It is 4.5 per cent per annum. Co-operative banks are allowed to pay an extra 0.5 per cent on its savings bank deposits.

**(b) Current Account Deposits:** These accounts are maintained by the people who need to have a liquid balance. Current account offers high liquidity. No interest is paid on current deposits and there are no restrictions on withdrawals from the current accounts. These accounts are generally in the case of proprietor, business firms, institutions and cooperative bodies. Nowadays, banks are designing and offering various investment schemes for deposit of money. Banks are currently working out with different innovative schemes for deposits. Such deposit accounts offer better interest rate and at the same time withdrawable facility also. These schemes are mostly offered by foreign banks. In USA, current accounts are known as 'Checking Accounts' as a cheque is equivalent to check in America.

**2. Accommodation of Loans and Advances:**

Commercial Bank attaches much importance to providing loans and advances at higher rates than the deposit rates and thus, earns profits on it. The commercial banks provide loans and advances in various forms. They are given below:

**(a) Overdraft:** This facility is given to holders of current accounts and nowadays it is giving facility on saving accounts also. This is an arrangement with the bankers wthereby the customer is allowed to withdraw money over and above the balance in his/her account. This facility of overdrawing his account is generally pre-arranged with the bank up to a certain limit. It is a short-term temporary fund facility from bank and the bank will charge interest over the amount overdrawn.

**(b) Cash Credit:** Cash credit is a form of working capital credit given to the business firms. Under this arrangement, the customer opens an account and the sanctioned amount is credited with that account. The customer can operate that account within the sanctioned limit as and when required.

It is made against security of goods, personal security, etc. On the basis of operation, the period of credit facility may be extended further. One advantage under this method is that bank charges interest only on the amount utilized and not on total amount sanctioned or credited to the account. Reserve Bank discourages this type of facility to business firms as it imposes an uncertainty on money supply. Hence, this method of lending is slowly phased out from banks and replaced by loan accounts. Mostly cash credit system is used in developing countries.

**(c) Loans and Advances:** It includes both demand and term loans. Similarly, direct loans and advances given to all types of customers mainly to businessmen and investors against personal security or goods of movable or immovable in nature. The loan amount is paid in cash or by credit to customer's account which the customer can draw at any time. The interest is charged for the full amount whether he withdraws the money from his account or not. Short-term loans are granted to meet the working capital requirements whereas long-term loans are granted to meet capital expenditure. Previously interest on loan was also regulated by RBI. Currently, banks can determine the rate themselves.

**Classification of Loans and Advances:**

Loans and advances given by bankers can be classified broadly into the following categories:

(i) Advances which are given on the personal security of the debtor, and for which no tangible or collateral security is taken. This type of advance is given either when the amount of the advance is very small, or when the borrower is known to the Banker and the Banker has complete confidence in him (Clean Advance).

(ii) Advances which are covered by tangible or collateral security. This type of advance with different types of securities which a Banker may accept is secured (Secured Advance).

(iii) Advances which are given against the personal security of the debtor but for which the Banker also holds in addition the guarantee of one or more sureties. This type of advance is often given by Banker to persons who are not known to them but whose surety is known to the Banker. Bankers also often take the personal guarantee of the Directors of a company to whom they agree to advance a clean or unsecured loan.

(iv) Loans are also given against the security of Fixed Deposit receipts.

**3. Credit Creation:**

Credit creation is one of the primary functions of commercial banks. Commercial Bank not only receives deposits from public and accommodates loans to public but also creates loan deposits. When a bank sanctions a loan to the customer, it does not give cash to him. But, a deposit account is opened in his name and the amount is credited to his account. He can withdraw the money whenever he needs. Thus, whenever a bank sanctions a loan it creates a deposit. In this way, the bank increases the money supply of the economy. Such functions are known as credit creation.

**Secondary Functions:**

The secondary functions of the banks consist of agency functions and general utility functions.

**1. Agency Functions:**

Agency functions include the following:

**(i) Collection of Cheques, Dividends, and Interests:** As an agent the bank collects cheques, drafts, promissory notes, interest, dividends, etc. On behalf of its customers and credit the amounts to their accounts. Customers may furnish their bank details to corporate where investment is made in shares, debentures, etc. as and when dividend, interest, is due, the companies directly send the warrants/cheques to the bank for credit to customer account.

**(ii) Payment of Rent, Insurance Premiums:** The bank makes the payments such as rent, insurance premiums, subscriptions on standing instructions until further notice. Till the order is revoked, the bank will continue to make such payments regularly by debiting the customer's account.

**(iii) Dealing in Foreign Exchange:** As an agent, the commercial banks purchase and sell foreign exchange as well for customers as per RBI Exchange Control Regulations.

**(iv) Purchase and Sale of Securities:** Commercial banks undertake the purchase and sale of different securities such as shares, debentures, bonds, etc., on behalf of their customers. They run a separate 'Portfolio Management Scheme' for their big customers.

**(v) Act as Trustee, Executor, Attorney, etc.:** The banks act as executors of Will, trustees and attorneys. It is safe to appoint a bank as a trustee than to appoint an individual. Acting as attorneys of their customers, they receive payments and sign transfer deeds of the properties of their customers.

**(vi) Act as Correspondent:** The commercial banks act as a correspondent of their customers. Small banks even get travel tickets, book vehicles, receive letters, etc. on behalf of the customers.

**(vii) Preparations of Income-Tax Returns:** They prepare income-tax returns and provide advices on tax matters for their customers. For this purpose, they employ tax experts and make their services available to their customers.

**(viii) Contribution in Foreign Trade:** Commercial Bank plays a vital role in expediting foreign exchange and foreign trade business e.g. import, export, etc. It contributes greatly in the economy through import finance and export finance and thus, earn foreign exchange for the country.

**(ix) Formation of Capital:** Commercial Bank extends financial assistance for the formation of capital in the trade, commerce and industry in the country which expedites its economic development.

**(x) Collection and Payment:** Commercial Bank is engaged in collection and payment of cheque, bill of exchange, promissory notes, pension, dividends, subscription, insurance premium, interest, etc. on behalf of the clients.

**(xi) Creation of Investment Environment:** Commercial Bank plays a significant role in creating investment environment in the country.

**(xii) Economic Development and Welfare Activities:** Commercial Bank contributes much for the welfare and economic development of the country.

**2. Public Utility Functions:**

In modern banking, commercial bank executes public utility services:

**(i) Remittance of Money:** Remittance of money to the public from one place to another is one of the functions of commercial bank. Remittance is effected in the form of demand draft, telegraphic transfer, etc. through different branches and correspondents, home and abroad.

**(ii) Safety Locker Facility:** Safekeeping of important documents, valuables like jewels are one of the oldest services provided by commercial banks. 'Lockers' are small receptacles which are fitted in steel racks and kept inside strong rooms known as vaults. These lockers are available on half-yearly or annual rental basis. The bank merely provides lockers and the key but the valuables are always under the control of its users. Any customer cannot have access to vault. Only customers of safety lockers after entering into a register his name, account number and time can enter into the vault. Because the vault is holding important valuables of customers in lockers, it is also known as 'Strong Room'.

**(iii) Payment Mechanism or Money Transfer:** Transfer of funds is one of the important functions performed by commercial banks. Cheques and credit cards are two important payment mechanisms through banks. Despite an increase in financial transactions, banks are managing the transfer of funds process very efficiently. Cheques are also cleared through the banking system. Correspondent banking is another method of transferring funds over long distance, usually from one country to another. Nowadays bank employ transfer of money by computer to reduce cost of transferring funds. Electronic Transfer of funds is also known as 'Chequeless banking' where funds are transferred through computers and sophisticated electronic system by using codewords. They offer Mail Transfer, Telegraphic Transfer (TT) facility also.

**(iv) Traveller's Cheques:** Traveller's Cheques are used by domestic traveller's as well as by international travellers. However, the use of traveller's cheques is more common by international travellers because of their safety and convenience. These can be also termed as a modified form of traveller's letter of credit. A bank issuing travellers cheques usually have banking arrangement with many of the foreign banks abroad known as correspondent banks. The purchaser of traveller's cheques can encash the cheques from all the overseas banks with whom the issuing bank has such an arrangement. The issuing bank levies certain commission depending upon the number and value of Travellers Cheques issued. Banks issue Travellers Cheques to help carry money safely while travelling within India or abroad. Thus, the customers can travel without fear, theft or loss of money.

(v) **Acting as Referees:** The banks act as referees and supply information about the business transactions and financial standing of their customers on enquiries made by third parties. This is done on the acceptance of the customers and help to increase the business activity in general.

(vi) **Help in trade and commerce:** Commercial Bank helps expand trade and commerce. Inland and foreign trade customers are allowed credit accommodation in the form of letter of credit , bill purchased and discounted, etc.

(vii) **Provides Trade Information:** The commercial banks collect information on business and financial conditions, etc., and make it available to their customers to help plan their strategy. Trade information service is very useful for those customers going for cross-border business. It will help traders to know the exact business conditions, payment rules and buyers' financial status in other countries.

(viii) **ATM facilities:** The banks today have ATM facilities. Under this system, the customers can withdraw their money easily and quickly and 24 hours a day. Under this system, customers can withdraw funds i.e. currency notes with the help of certain magnetic card issued by the bank and similarly deposit cash/ cheque for crediting to his account.

(ix) **Credit Cards:** Banks have introduced credit card system. Credit cards enable a customer to purchase goods and services from certain specified retail and service establishments upto a limit without making immediate payment. In other words, purchases can be made on credit basis on the strength of the credit card. The establishments like Hotels, Shops, Airline Companies, Railways, etc. which sell the goods or services on credit forward a monthly or fortnightly statements to the bank. The amount is paid to these establishment by the bank. The bank subsequently collects the dues from the customers by debit to their accounts. Usually, the bank receives certain service charges for every credit card issued. Visa Card, BOB card are some examples of credit cards.

(x) **Gift Cheques:** The commercial banks offer Gift cheque facilities to the general public. These cheques have received a wider acceptance in India. Under this system by paying equivalent amount one can buy gift cheque for presentation on occasions like Wedding, Birthday, etc.

(xi) **Accepting Bills:** On behalf of their customers, banks accept bills drawn by third parties on its customers. This resembles the letter of credit. While banks accept bills, they provide a better security for payment to seller of goods or drawer of bills.

(xii) **Merchant Banking:** The commercial banks provide valuable services through their merchant banking divisions or through their subsidiaries to the traders. This is the function of underwriting of securities. They underwrite a portion of the Public issue of shares, Debentures and Bonds of Joint Stock Companies. Such underwriting ensures the expected minimum subscription and also convey to the investing public about the quality of the company issuing the securities. Currently, this type of services can be provided only by separate subsidiaries known as Merchant Bankers as per SEBI regulations.

(xiii) **Advice on Financial Matters:** The commercial banks also give advice to their customers on financial matters particularly on investment decisions such as expansion, diversification, new ventures, rising of funds, etc.

(xiv) **Factoring Service:** Today, the commercial banks provide factoring service to their customers. It is very much helpful in the development of trade and industry as immediate cash flow and administration of debtors' accounts are taken care of by factors. This service is again provided only by a separate subsidiary as per RBI regulations.

(xv) **Act as an Adviser:** Commercial Bank provides valuable advice to the customers on different products, business growth and development, feasibility of business and industry.

(xvi) **Collect Utility Service Bills:** As a social commitment, Commercial Bank collects utility service bills e.g. water, electricity, gas, telephone, etc. from the public.

**(xvii) Purchase and Sale of Prize Bonds, SanchayaPatra, Shares, etc.:** Commercial Bank undertakes to purchase and sale of prize bonds, sanchayapatra, shares, etc. as a part of social commitment.

### 2.1.3 Phases of Banking in India

#### (A) First Phase : 1948-1969:

The country inherited a banking system that was patterned on the British Banking System. There were many joint stock companies doing banking business and they were concentrating mostly in major cities. Even the financing activities of these banks were confined to the exports of Jute, Tea, etc. and traditional industries like textile and sugar. There was no uniform law governing banking activity. An immediate concern after the partition of the country was about bank branches located in Pakistan and steps were taken to close some of them as desired by that country. In 1949, as many as 55 banks either went into liquidation or went out of banking business. Banking did not receive much attention of the policy makers and disjointed efforts were made towards the regulation of the banking industry.

#### (B) Second Phase : Nationalization Era: 1969-1990:

#### B.1 Nationalization:

By the 1960s, the Indian banking industry had become an important tool to facilitate the development of the Indian economy. Indira Gandhi, the-then Prime Minister of India expressed the intention of the Government of India (GOI) about Bank Nationalization, her move was swift and sudden, and the GOI issued an ordinance and nationalized the 14 largest commercial banks with effect from the midnight of July 19, 1969. The Parliament passed the Banking Companies (Acquisition and Transfer of Undertaking) Bill, and it received the presidential approval on 9 August, 1969. A second step of nationalization of 6 more commercial banks followed in1980. The stated reason for the nationalization was to give the government more control of credit delivery. With the second step of nationalization, the GOI controlled around 91% of the banking business in India. Later on, in the year 1993, the government merged New Bank of India with Punjab National Bank. It was the only merger between nationalized banks and resulted in the reduction of the number of nationalized banks from 20 to 19. After this, until the 1990s, the nationalized banks grew at a pace of around 4%, closer to the average growth rate of the Indian economy.

**14 Major Banks which were Nationalized:**

1. The Central Bank of India Ltd.
2. The Bank of India Ltd.
3. The Punjab National Bank Ltd.
4. The Bank of Baroda Ltd.
5. The United Commercial Bank Ltd.
6. The Canara Bank Ltd.
7. The United Bank of India Ltd.
8. The Dena Bank Ltd.
9. Syndicate Bank Ltd.
10. The Union Bank of India Ltd.
11. The Allahabad Bank Ltd.
12. The Indian Bank Ltd.
13. The Bank of Maharashtra Ltd.
14. The Indian Overseas Bank Ltd.

Each bank was having deposits of more than ₹ 50 crore and having among themselves aggregate deposits of ₹ 2632 crore with 4130 branches. On 15$^{th}$ April 1980, six more banks were nationalized. Each bank was having deposits of more than ₹ 200 crore. These banks were:

1. The Andhra Bank Ltd.,
2. The Corporation Bank Ltd.,
3. The New Bank of India Ltd.,
4. The Oriental Bank of Commerce Ltd.,
5. The Punjab and Sind Bank Ltd.,
6. The Vijya Bank Ltd.

There were some effects and achievements of nationalized banks. However, there were some problems relating to NPAs, competition, competency, overstaffing, inefficiency, etc. for the nationalized banks.

**(C) Third Phase (Economic Reforms) : 1991-2002:**

The Indian economic development took place in the realistic world from 1991 because of "New Economic Policy" include "Liberalization, Privatization and Globalization" policy. As per "LPG" policy, all restrictions on the Indian economy were totally dissolved and the soundest phase for the Indian banking system adopted over here. This also changed the scenario of the macro-economic world. The budget policy and suggestion provided by Dr. Man Mohan Singh and the Governor of Reserve Bank of India. The country is flooded with foreign banks and their ATM stations. Efforts are being put to give a satisfactory service to customers. Phone banking and net banking have been introduced. The entire system became more convenient and swift. Time is given more importance than money. The financial system of India has shown a great deal of resilience. It is sheltered from any crisis triggered by any external macro-economics shock as other East Asian countries suffered. This is all due to a flexible exchange rate regime, the foreign reserves are high, the capital account is not yet fully convertible, and banks and their customers have limited foreign exchange exposure.

### 2.1.4 Reforms in Banking Sector in India

Banking Sector reforms were initiated to upgrade the operating standard health and financial soundness of the banks. The Government of India set up the Narasimham Committee in 1991 to examine all aspects relating to structure, organization and functioning of the Indian banking system. The recommendations of the committee aimed at creating at competitive and efficient banking system. Another committee which is Khan Committee was instituted by RBI in December, 1997 to examine the harmonization of the role and operations of development of financial institutions and banks. It submitted its report in 1998. The major recommendations were a gradual move towards universal banking, exploring the possibility of gainful merger between banks and financial institutions Then the Verma Committee was established. This committee recommended the need for greater use of IT even in the weak public sector banks, restructuring of weak banks but not merging them with strong banks, VRS for at least 25% of the staff. The Banking sector reforms aimed at improving the policy frame work, financial health and institutional infrastructure, there two phase of the banking reforms. Narasimham Committee provided the blue print for the initial reforms in the banking sector.

**Phase I : Recommendations of Narasimham Committee 1991**

- Deregulation of the interest rate structure
- Progressive reduction in pre-emptive reserves
- Liberalization of the branch expansion policy
- Introduction of prudential norms
- Deregulation of the entry norms for private sector banks
- Permitting public and private sector banks to access the capital market
- Setting up to asset reconstruction fund
- Constituting the special debt recovery tribunals
- Freedom to appoint chief executive and officers of the banks
- Changes in the institutions of the board
- Bringing NBFC under the ambit of regulatory framework.

**Phase II: Narsimham Committee (Capital Adequacy) II April 1998**

- Minimum capital to risk asset ratio be increased from the existing 8 percent to 10 percent by 2002
- 100 percent of fixed income portfolio marked to market by 2001
- 5 percent market risk weight for fixed income securities and open foreign exchange position limits
- Commercial risk weight (100%) to government guaranteed.

### 2.1.5 Structure of Indian Banking System

The structure of banking varies widely from country to country. The banking system in India works under the constraints that go with social control and public ownership. The Indian financial system comprises a large number of commercial and cooperative banks, specialized developmental banks for industry, agriculture, external trade and housing, social security institutions, collective investment institutions, etc. The banking system is at the heart of the financial system. The Indian banking system has the RBI at the apex. It is the central bank of the country under which there are the commercial banks including public sector and private sector banks, foreign banks and local area banks. It also includes regional rural banks as well as cooperative banks.

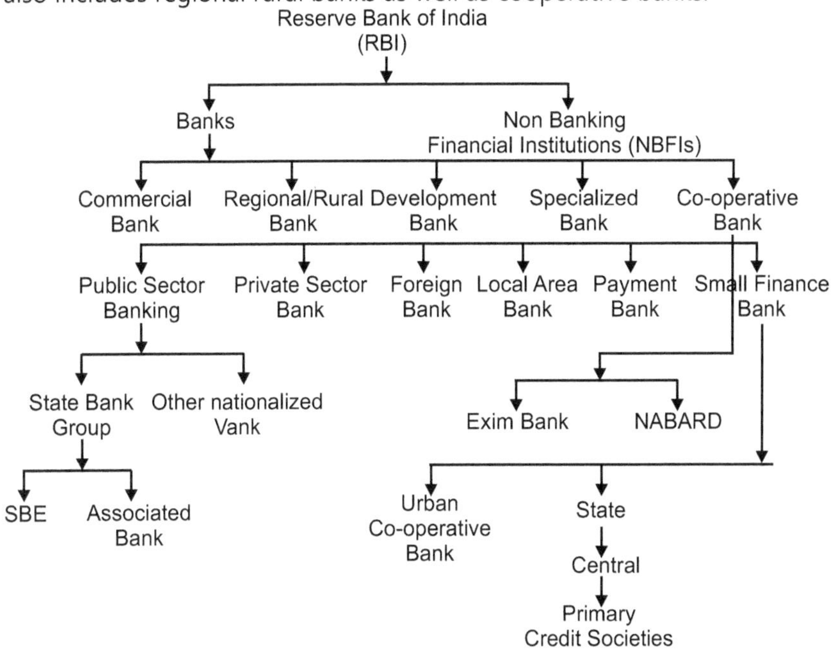


**Fig. 2.1: Structure of Indian Banking System**

The recommendations of some of these Expert Committees favoured consolidation in the Indian banking structure to create well-capitalised, automated and technology-oriented banks through mergers and acquisitions; fostering competition in the banking structure through permitting more private sector banks; setting up of small banks with local character to cater to the requirements of rural and unorganised sectors; more active foreign banks participation; strengthening of the existing structure through enhancing appropriate risk management capabilities; and putting in place legal, insurance, resolution and prudential measures to enable the banking structure to discharge its core functions in an efficient and inclusive manner.

**Reserve Bank of India (RBI):**

The central bank plays an important role in the monetary and banking structure of a nation. It supervises, controls and regulates the activities of the banking sector. It has been assigned to handle and control the currency and credit of a country. The RBI is India's central bank. The RBI was established on April 1, 1935 in accordance with the provisions of the Reserve Bank of India Act, 1934. It was a private shareholders institution till January 1949, after which it became a state-owned institution under the Reserve Bank of India Act, 1948. It has been guiding, monitoring, regulating and promoting the destiny of the Indian financial system. RBI acts as a banker to the Government and Banks. The Central Bank maintains record of Government revenue and expenditure under various heads. It maintains deposit accounts of all other banks and advances money to other banks when needed. Another important function of the Central Bank is the issuance of currency notes and regulating their circulation in the country by different methods. Banks in the country are broadly classified as scheduled banks and non-scheduled banks.

**Scheduled Banks:**

All banks which are included in the Second Schedule to the Reserve Bank of India Act, 1934 are scheduled banks. These banks comprise Scheduled Commercial Banks and Scheduled Cooperative Banks. These banks are eligible for certain facilities such as financial accommodation from RBI and are required to fulfill certain statutory obligations. The RBI is empowered to exclude any bank from the schedule whose:

(1) Aggregate value of paid up capital and reserves fall below ₹ 5 lakh.

(2) Affairs are conducted in a manner detrimental to the interests of depositors.

(3) Goes into liquidation and ceases to transact banking business

**Commercial Banks:**

Amongst the banking institutions in the organized sector, commercial banks are the oldest institutions, some of them having their genesis in the nineteenth century. Initially, they were set up in large numbers, mostly as corporate bodies with shareholdings by private individuals. Commercial banks may be defined as, any banking organization that deals with the deposits and loans of business organizations. Commercial banks issue bank checks and drafts, as well as accept money on term deposits. Commercial banks also act as money lenders by way of instalment loans and overdrafts. Commercial banks also allow for a variety of deposits. These institutions are run to make profit and owned by a group of individuals.

**Public Sector Banks:**

These are banks where majority stake is held by the Government of India. Public sector in Indian banking emerged to its present position in three stages. First, the conversion of the then existing Imperial Bank of India into the State Bank of India in 1955, followed by the taking over of the seven state associated banks as its subsidiary banks, second the nationalization of 14 major commercial banks on July 19, 1969 and last, the nationalization of 6 more commercial banks on April 15, 1980. There were 27 banks constituting public sector banks. However in September 2019, government of India announced merger of eight public sector banks in other public sector banks.

**Foreign Banks:**

These banks are registered and have their headquarters in a foreign country but operate their branches in our country. Foreign Commercial Banks are the branches in India of the joint stock banks incorporated abroad. These banks, besides financing the foreign trade of the country, undertake normal banking business in the country as well. They have made substantial inroads in internal trade including deposits, advances, discounting of bills, mutual funds, ATMs and credit cards. A large part of their credit is extended to large enterprises and MNCs located mostly in the metro cities, though some banks are now foraying in the rural sector as well. Technology used by these banks has been a major driver of change in the Indian banking industry. A highly trained and efficient workforce and the huge pool of capital resources at the disposal of these banks have created tremendous goodwill and prestige in India. In 2012, there were 41 foreign banks and their 323 branches functioning in India.

**Private Sector Banks:**

After the nationalization of major banks in the private sector in 1969 and 1980, no new bank could be set up in India for about two decades, though there was no legal bar to that effect. The Narasimham Committee on Financial Sector Reforms recommended the establishment of new banks in India. Reserve Bank of India, thereafter, issued guidelines for the setting up of new private sector banks in India in January 1993. These guidelines aimed at ensuring that the new banks were financially viable and technologically up-to-date from the start. They had to function in a professional manner, so as to improve the image of commercial banking system and to win the confidence of the public. In January 2001, Reserve Bank of India issued new rules for the licensing of new banks in the private sector. These those banks majority of share capital of which were held by private individuals. These banks were registered as companies with limited liability.

**Regional Rural Banks:**

Regional Rural Banks were established under the provisions of an ordinance promulgated in September 1975 and the RRB Act, 1976 with an objective to ensure sufficient institutional credit for agriculture and other rural sectors. The area of operation of RRBs is limited to the area as notified by Government of India covering one or more districts in the state. RRBs are jointly owned by Government of India, the concerned State Government and Sponsor Banks (27 Scheduled commercial banks and one State Cooperative Bank); the issued capital of a RRB is shared by the owners in the proportion of 50%, 15% and 35% respectively. Prathama bank is the first Regional Rural Bank is India located in the city Moradabad in Uttar Pradesh.

**Cooperative Banks:**

The cooperative banks have been set up under the various Co-operative Societies Acts enacted by the State Governments. Hence, the State Governments regulate these banks. In 1966, need was felt to regulate their activities to ensure their soundness and to protect the interests of depositors. Consequently, certain provisions of the Banking Regulation Act, 1949 were made applicable to co-operative banks as well. These banks have thus fallen under dual control viz. that of the State

Govt. and that of the Reserve Bank of India which exercises control over them so far as their banking operations are concerned. A cooperative bank is a financial entity which belongs to its members who are at the same time the owners and the customers of their bank. Cooperative banks are often created by persons belonging to the same local or professional community or sharing a common interest. Co-operative banks generally provide their members with a wide range of banking and financial services (loans, deposits, banking and accounts, etc.). They provide limited banking products and are specialists in agriculture-related products. Cooperative banks are the primary financiers of agricultural activities, some small-scale industries and self employed workers. Cooperative banks function on the basis of "no-profit no-loss". The Co-operative Credit system consists of (a) Short-term agricultural credit institutions, (b) Long-term agricultural credit institutions and (c) Non-agricultural credit institutions.

**Local Area Bank:**

In 1996, Government decided to allow new local area banks with the twin objectives of providing an institutional mechanism for promoting rural and semi-urban savings, and for providing credit for viable, economic activities in the local areas. Such banks can be established as public limited companies in the private sector and can be promoted by individuals, companies, trusts and societies. The minimum paid up capital of such banks would be ₹ 5 crore with promoter's contribution of at least ₹ 2 crore. They are to be set up in district towns and the area of their operations would be limited to a maximum of 3 geographically contiguous districts. In 2010, five Local Area Banks were functional, one each in Punjab, Gujarat, Maharashtra and two in Andhra Pradesh.

**Export-Import Bank of India (EXIM BANK):**

Export-Import Bank of India is the premier export finance institution of the country, established in 1982 under the Export-Import Bank of India Act, 1981.

**Industrial Development Bank of India (IDBI):**

On 16$^{th}$ February 1976, the ownership of IDBI was transferred to the Government of India and it was made the principal financial institution for coordinating the activities of institutions engaged in financing, promoting and developing industry in the country.

**National Bank for Agriculture and Rural Development (NABARD):**

NABARD is an apex development bank in India having headquarters based in Mumbai (Maharashtra) and other branches all over the country. It was established on 12$^{th}$ July 1982 on the recommendations of Shivaram

Committee, by an act of parliament on 12th July 1982 to implement the National Bank for Agriculture and Rural Development Act, 1981.

**Private Banks in India:**

The private-sector banks in India represent part of the Indian banking sector. The private-sector banks are banks where greater parts of stake or equity is held by the private shareholders and not by government. Private sector banks are the banks that are controlled by the private lenders with the approval from the Reserve Bank of India (RBI). Their interest rates are slightly expensive as compared to Public sector banks.

Banking in India has been dominated by public sector banks since the 1969 when all major banks were nationalized by the Indian government. However, since liberalization, banking policy in 1990s, old and new private sector banks have re-emerged. They have grown faster and bigger over the two decades since liberalization using the latest technology, providing contemporary innovations and monetary tools and techniques. Private-sector banks have been functioning in India since the very beginning of the banking system. Initially, during 1921, the private banks like Bank of Bengal, Bank of Bombay and Bank of Madras were in service, which together formed Imperial Bank of India. Reserve Bank of India (RBI) came in picture in 1935 and became the centre of every other bank taking away all the responsibilities and functions of the Imperial Bank. Between 1969 and 1980, there was rapid increase in the number of branches of the private banks. In April 1980, they accounted for nearly 17.5 percent of bank branches in India. In 1980, after 6 more banks were nationalized, about 10 percent of the bank branches were those of private-sector banks. The share of the private bank branches stayed nearly same between 1980 and 2000. Then from the early 1990s, RBI's liberalization policy came in picture and with this the government gave licenses to a few private banks, which came to be known as new private-sector banks. There are two categories of the private-sector banks: "old" and "new". The old private-sector banks have been operating since a long time and may be referred to as those banks, which are in operation from before 1991 and all those banks that have commenced their business after 1991 are called as new private sector banks. Housing Development Finance Corporation Limited (HDFC) was the first private bank in India to receive license from RBI.

**Reserve Bank of India's New Policy for Private Banks:**

The Narasimham Committee-I, that advocated competition in the banking industry, made unequivocal recommendation to allow private and foreign banks into the industry. Acting on the recommendations of the committee, the RBI laid down guidelines for the establishment of the private sector banks in January 1993. The guidelines prescribed that the private banks should be established as public limited companies under the Indian Companies Act, 1956. In January 2001, Reserve Bank of India issued new rules for the licensing of new banks in the private sector. The salient features are as follows:

1. A new bank may be started with a capital of ₹ 200 crore. The net worth is to be raised to ₹ 300 crore in three years.
2. The promoter's minimum holding in the capital shall be 40 per cent with a lock-in-period of 5 years. Excess holding over 40 per cent will have to be diluted within a year.
3. Non-resident Indians can pick up 40 per cent equity share in the new bank. Any foreign bank or finance company may join as technical collaborators or as co-promoter, but their equity participation will be restricted to 20 per cent, which will be within the ceiling of 40 per cent allowed to Non-resident Indians.
4. Corporates have been allowed to invest up to meeting existing priority sector norms and prudential norms and also to open 25 % of their branches in rural and semi-urban areas. Preference will be given to promoters with expertise in financing priority areas and rural and agro-based industries.
5. Non-banking finance companies may convert themselves into banks if their net worth is ₹ 200 crore, capital adequacy ratio is 12%, non performing assets below 5% and possess triple A credit rating.

Accordingly, nine banks were set-up in private sector including some by development financial institutions. Prominent among them were ICICI Bank, GTB, HDFC and IDBI Bank. Another interesting development was merger of some banks. Bareily Corporation Ltd merged with Bank of Baroda in 1999, Times Bank merged with HDFC Bank in 1996, Bank of Madura Ltd. merged with ICICI Bank in 2001 and Nedungadi Bank Ltd merged with Punjab National Bank in 2003. The New Private Sector Banks started publishing balance sheets since 1995-96.

**Foreign Investment:**

The Government has been pursuing an open door policy and opened the floodgates for the inflow of foreign capital in the form of FOI, investments by foreign institutional investors and NRIs in the banking sector too. Foreign investments in private banks from all sources (FOI, FII, NRI), which was limited to 49 per cent of the capital but now raised to 74 percent facilitating setting up of subsidiaries of foreign banks and attracting investment in private sector banks. The new private sector banks are allowed to raise capital contribution from foreign institutional investors up to 20 per cent and from NRIs up to 40 percent of their share capital. Promoter's stake in Indian banks is currently limited to 49 per cent. While issuing licenses, the RBI has instructed those promoters of private banks who held a higher holding than the prescribed limit to divest their stake and bring it down to 49 percent. Indian promoters argue that such discrimination may make Indian private banks vulnerable to take-over by foreign banks. It is hoped that the limit to Indian promoters holding will be raised to 74 per cent as is done for FOI.

**Types of Private Sector Banks:**

Broadly, there are four types of private banks in India.

**(i) Old Generation Private Banks**

The banks, which were not nationalized at the time of bank nationalization that took place during 1969 and 1980s are known to be the old private-sector banks. These were not nationalized because of their small size and regional focus. Most of the old private-sector banks are closely held by certain communities and their operations are mostly restricted to the areas in and around their place of origin. Their Board of Directors mainly consist of locally prominent personalities from trade and business circles. One of the positive points of these banks is that, they lean heavily on service and technology and as such, they are likely to attract more business in days to come with the restructuring of the industry round the corner. e.g. Bank of Rajasthan Ltd., City Union Bank Ltd., Dhanalakshmi Bank Ltd., Federal Bank Ltd., Karnataka Bank Ltd., etc.

**(ii) New Generation Private-Sector Banks:**

The banks, which came in operation after 1991, with the introduction of economic reforms and financial sector reforms are called "new private-sector banks". Banking Regulation Act was then amended in 1993, which permitted the entry of new private-sector banks in the Indian banking sector. However, there were certain criteria set for the establishment of the new private-sector banks, some of those criteria being: The bank should have a minimum net worth of ₹ 200 crores.

(1) The promoters holding should be a minimum of 25% of the paid-up capital.

(2) Within 3 years of the starting of the operations, the bank should offer shares to public and their net worth must be increased to 300 crores. e.g. HDFC Bank Ltd., ICICI Bank Ltd. IndusInd Bank Ltd., Kotak Mahindra Bank Ltd., Axis Bank, Yes Bank Ltd., etc.

**(iii) Foreign Banks Operating in India:**

In 2005, the Reserve Bank released the road map for presence of foreign banks in India laying out a two track and gradualist approach aimed at increasing the efficiency and stability of the banking sector in India. One track was the consolidation of the domestic banking system, both in private and public sectors, and the second track was the gradual enhancement of foreign banks in a synchronized manner. The road map was divided into two phases, the first phase spanning the period March 2005 – March 2009 and the second phase beginning after a review of the experience gained in the first phase. However, when the time came to review the experience gained in the first phase, global financial markets were in turmoil and there were uncertainties surrounding the financial strength of banks around the world. At that time, it was considered advisable to continue with the current policy and procedures governing the presence of foreign banks in India. Foreign banks present in India as representative offices often have correspondent banking relationships with domestic banks and provide a useful platform for foreign banks to access opportunities for foreign currency lending to Indian corporates and financial institutions.

**(iv) Co-operative Banks in India:**

Under 1904 Act, only primary credit societies were permitted to register and 1912 Co-operative Societies Act bridged for noncredit and federal organisations of primary co-operative credit societies. But the provisions of 1912 Act were inadequate to meet the requirements of those states where co-operative movement had made considerable progress. Hence, in this regard a new Act was passed viz. the Bombay Cooperative Societies Act, 1925 for serving the many sided development of the state. Later on, Madras, Bihar and Bengal passed their own Acts in 1932, 1935 and 1940 respectively.

India's co-operative banking structure consists of two main segments, viz., agricultural and non-agricultural credit. There are two separate structures in the case of agricultural credit - one for short and medium term credit and the other for long term credit. The co-operative credit structure for short and medium terms is a three-tier one with primary agricultural credit societies at the base level, the central co-operative bank at the district level and state co-operative bank at the apex level. Over and above these institutions, grain banks are actively functioning as primary societies in certain states. Though the organisation of central and state co-operative banks was mainly for the benefit of the agricultural credit sector, they serve nonagricultural societies too.

**Financial Performance of Commercial Private Sector Banks in India:**

The performance of Old Private Banks (OPBs) and 8 New Private Banks (NPBs) was evaluated during the reform period. The 8 new private bank as has already been stated, came into existence after 1992-93 and the financial results of these banks were published from 1995-96. Hence, their performance analysis rebates to the period 2008-09 to 2012-13 showed in following table.

**Table 2.1 : Financial Performance of Commercial Private Sector Banks in India (₹ in million)**

| Year | Number of Banks | Number of Offices | Employees | Capital and Reserve and Surplus | Deposits | Investments | Advances | Interest Income | Other income |
|---|---|---|---|---|---|---|---|---|---|
| 2008-09 | 22 | 9288 | 193578 | 996686 | 7363776 | 3065312 | 5753276 | 850714 | 178602 |
| 2009-10 | 22 | 10516 | 188332 | 1199839 | 8228007 | 3541169 | 6324409 | 828064 | 204231 |
| 2010-11 | 21 | 12097 | 248284 | 1385664 | 10027588 | 4220576 | 7975440 | 967131 | 208734 |
| 2011-12 | 20 | 13970 | 269941 | 1592952 | 11745874 | 5259822 | 9664030 | 1345555 | 250480 |
| 2012-13 | 20 | 16001 | - | 1929461 | 13958355 | 6261063 | 11432486 | 1664864 | 297927 |

**Source:** https://www.rbi.org.in/Scripts/AnnualPublication

Following table 2.2 shows that the key bank metrics of the selected banks in 2017.

**Table 2.2: Bank Metrics (₹ in Billion)**

| Bank | Market Cap | Net Interest Income | Net Profit | Total Assets |
|---|---|---|---|---|
| HDFC | 4254 | 693 | 146 | 7088 |
| ICICI | 1860 | 542 | 98 | 7718 |
| Kotak | 1812 | 177 | 34 | 2146 |
| Axis | 1239 | 445 | 37 | 6015 |
| IndusInd | 891 | 144 | 29 | 1401 |

**Source:** https://www.researchgate.net/publication

**Modern Trends in Private Sector Banks:**

Some of the key trends that will shape the future of Indian banking are:

**(i) Focus on retail banking:** Rapid accumulation of wealth in households and emergence of the billion consumers segment would drive growth in retail banking, both for high net worth individuals, as well as for the emerging middle class.

**(ii) Increasing banking footprint:** Banks will have to expand their networks extensively by setting up branches and ATMs. The industry will follow the model of low–cost branch network, involving smaller sized branches.

**(iii) Lower margins:** The sector would face downward pressure on margins in retail as well as corporate banking. Banks will invest in innovative technologies to improve efficiency and lower costs.

**(iv) Financial inclusion:** Financial inclusion, which requires banks to come up with innovative solutions to cater to low ticket–size customers, is a central item on the Government's agenda. The Ministry of Finance has mandated public sector banks to focus on financial inclusion. At the same time, private banks have also started focussing on this. The current business models are not economically viable, and new models such as the business correspondent approach will have to be radically different in terms of distribution, technology, HR practices and risk management.

**(v) IT and Banking Sector:** IT will play a critical role in the growth of the banking sector. The larger banks have successfully implemented the basic IT infrastructure required to run their operations, and the next tier is also moving towards greater IT adoption through increased outsourcing of its IT functions. Larger investments would be needed to upgrade existing systems and develop new ones to meet the growing and ever–changing business requirements.

(vi) **Management:** Banks are expected to spend on upgrading their IT systems to make their internal processes efficient and cost-effective. Future IT spends will include: Use of cloud computing to improve efficiency, reduced costs and scale up operations without incurring additional expenses on hardware, software and manpower–implementation of tools for better HR management, especially in PSU banks–Migration to paperless transactions and processing, such as cheque truncation system-increased investments in areas such as automated data flow, data storage as per KYC norms and document management, to ensure compliance with regulations.

(vii) **Data Warehousing:** To manage the growing volume of business transactions, banks would increasingly spend on data warehousing that can enable efficient decision making by providing a repository of historical data through systematic design. This would require a vast suite of applications, giving rise to multiple opportunities for IT providers.

(viii) **E–Payments and Mobile Banking:** For the next generation of tech–savvy customers, mobile is emerging as the preferred medium of conducting banking transactions. Private banks are developing capabilities to provide mobile banking services to their customers. Nationalized banks, too, are starting to adopt this technology. Going forward, banks will invest in development of systems and applications that will cater to the demand for such services from the new breed of technology–friendly customers, helping banks to build lasting client relationships.

(ix) **Payment Systems:** An increasing portfolio of products across delivery channels, coupled with newer methods of making payments, would require banks to invest in development of new payment systems to ensure protection of customer funds and internal security.

(x) **ATM Outsourcing:** Another major opportunity for IT providers lies in the ATM space. The rollout of ATMs is on the rise to cater to the population in tier 2 and tier 3 cities. There is an increasing trend towards outsourcing of ATM management, with many banks embracing total outsourcing models, which encompasses management of installation, ATM services as well as assets.

**(xi) Regulations:** One of the important drivers of IT spending by banks will be the guidelines put forth by RBI that pertain to the use of IT. RBI's guidelines for banks include greater use of technology with regard to upgrades in RRBs, KYC norms and the cheque truncation system.

**Advantages of Private Sector Banks:**

The importance of private sector in Indian economy over the last 15 years has been tremendous. The opening up of Indian economy has led to free inflow of foreign direct investment (FDI) along with modern cutting edge technology, which increased the importance of private sector in Indian economy considerably.

(i) Increased quality of life
(ii) Increased access to essential items
(iii) Increased production opportunities
(iv) Lowered prices of essential items
(v) Increased value of human capital
(vi) Improved social life of the middle class Indian
(vii) Decreased the percentage of people living below the poverty line in India
(viii) Changed the age old perception of poor agriculture based country to a rising manufacturing based country
(ix) Effected increased research and development activity and spending
(x) Effected better higher education facilities especially in technical fields
(xi) Ensured fair competition amongst market players
(xii) Dissolved the concept of monopoly and thus, neutralized market manipulation practices

**Small Banks in India:**

Small banks play a very important role in the supply of credit to small business units, small farmers and other unorganized sector entities. The need and the relevance of small banks has been debated in India from time to time and accordingly, various initiatives were put in place to promote small banks geared towards small borrowers. The small finance banks shall be registered as a public limited company under the Companies Act, 2013. It will be licensed under Section 22 of the Banking Regulation Act, 1949 and governed by the provisions of the Banking Regulation Act, 1949.

**Objectives:**

The objectives of setting up of small finance banks will be for furthering financial inclusion by:

(i) Provision of savings vehicles primarily to unserved and underserved sections of the population, and

(ii) Supply of credit to small business units; small and marginal farmers; micro and small industries; and other unorganised sector entities, through high technology-low cost operations

**Cross-Country Experience:**

The United States has got a banking structure comprising both big banking institutions, hand in hand, with small community banks focusing on specific geographical areas. Small community banks form a very important segment of the US banking system, though they account for a very small share of the total banking assets of the country. These banks are closely tied to the local communities and focus on mainly 'relationship banking'. In the US, there are about 7,000 small community banks with asset size ranging from less than US $10 million to US $10 billion or more. They account for about 46 per cent of all small loans to businesses and farms and in terms of the number, they constitute about 92 per cent of the all the FDIC insured institutions (FDIC, 2013). Enactment of the Mutual Banks Act of 1993 in South Africa was an attempt to add depth to the financial system by creating a banking category that had less stringent capital adequacy prerequisites but similar risk management requirements. In Nigeria, over 1,400 community banks were set up in both rural and urban areas. In Indonesia, the banking system is multifarious, with simultaneous existence of commercial banks in big cities, branches of provincial banks in small towns, the Unit Desa (village banks) of Bank Rakyat Indonesia (BRI), the local small banks, cooperative banks and private rural banks.

**Indian Experience with Small Banks:**

**Experience with LABs:**

An announcement by the then Finance Minister in the August 1996 Budget, the concept of Local Area Banks (LABs) was conceived as low cost structures and for providing efficient and competitive financial intermediation services in their areas of operation in the rural and semi-urban areas. The scheme envisaged a Local Area Bank with a minimum capital of ₹ 5 crore and an area of operation comprising three contiguous districts. Six LABs were licensed by RBI, of which 2 were closed down and only 4 are functioning. The overall performance of functioning LABs is less than satisfactory as they have become high cost structures. The cost income ratios of the 4 LABs ranged from 58.24 per cent to 87.20 per cent as on March 31, 2012. The LAB model has inherent weaknesses owing to their small size and concentration risk. This has resulted in unviable and uncompetitive cost structures, adverse selection, constraints in attracting and retaining professional staff/management due to locational disadvantage.

**Experience with UCBs and Other Small Banks:**

There has been a phenomenal growth in the UCB sector since 1966 in terms of number of banks, volume of banking business (deposits plus loans and advances) and geographical outreach. At the same time, low capital base, lack of professional management, poor credit management and diversion of funds have led to multi-faceted problems. In the absence of technology platform in the UCBs, they have not been able to leverage their potential for financial inclusion.

**Views of Financial Sector Reforms Committee on Small Banks in India:**

The Committee on Financial Sector Reforms (Chairman: Dr. Raghuram G. Rajan), 2009 examined the relevance of small banks in the Indian context. The Committee opined that there has been sufficient change in the environment to warrant experimentation with licensing small banks. In view of the fact that the failure of even a few small banks will not have systemic consequences, it recommended allowing more entry to private well-governed deposit-taking small finance banks (SFBs) offsetting their higher risk from being geographically focused by requiring higher capital adequacy norms, a strict prohibition on related party transactions and lower allowable concentration norms. Further, the committee suggested implementation of a strong prompt corrective action regime so that unviable cooperatives are closed and recommended that well-run cooperatives with a good track record explore conversion to a small bank, with members becoming shareholders.

The committee suggested the following features for small banks:

(i) Small banks should have some leeway to decide where they will grow and what they will focus on.

(ii) It would be appropriate to restrict the initial license to a certain maximum number of branches and asset size, with these restrictions removed after a review of performance.

(iii) To facilitate appropriate diversification and smaller loan ticket sizes, their exposure limits would be set at a lower fraction of capital than for SCBs, allowing them to increase ticket sizes as they grow.

(iv) Initial total required capital should be kept at a low level, consistent with the initial intent behind LABs.

**Merits and Demerits of Small Bank:**

**Merits:**

(i) Small banks have a small capital base and therefore lend to small borrowers.

(ii) Banks with limited area of operation would require less infrastructure and staff and, hence, the operational expenses would be low.

(iii) Small banks would help improve penetration of banking sector to unbanked areas and mobilize resources.

(iv) Such banks are expected to extend basic banking services and therefore, would attract people of small means who would require basic banking services.

(v) Their operations are confined to a district or few contiguous districts and hence they would be in a better position to understand the needs and priorities in their area of operation. They would be able to explore business potential more tailored to the socio economic background in the area of operation and extend banking services to the people in that area. For instance, community banks in the US transform local deposits into loans to communities where depositors live and work (Daniel Tarullo, 2010).

(vi) Small banks may develop core competence through relationship banking in financing agriculture, SMEs, industries in a particular geographical area and, thereby, able to serve their credit needs better.

(vii) Small banks have simple structures. Their failure will have less contagion effects and resolution would be easier.

(viii) Small banks have a comparative advantage in the supply of credit to small business units, small farmers and other unorganized sector entities, thereby furthering the cause of financial inclusion.

(ix) Small local banks are more nimble and flexible. They can effectively cater to unbanked areas and meet localized needs. Can be more efficient in financial inclusion.

(x) Failure of a small bank will not have any systemic impact and resolution would be easier.

**Demerits:**

(i) Small banks have the potential for financial inclusion, performance of the small banks in India (LABs, RRBs and UCBs) has been unsatisfactory. There are fundamental weaknesses inherent in the business model of small banks, such as narrow capital base, restrictive geographical jurisdiction, lack of diversification in source of funds.

(ii) Small banks are potentially vulnerable to sector and geographical concentration risk. For instance, community banks in the US suffered losses due to their excessive reliance on lending to commercial real estate (Daniel Tarullo, 2010).

(iii) Small banks are vulnerable to shocks from the local economy.

(iv) Small banks cannot finance big-ticket investments, including infrastructure.

(v) They lack economies of scale and scope.

(vi) Small banks are prone to capture by local influence.

(vii) There are some recent studies arguing that instead of relationship banking, which is generally followed by small banks, lending practices adopted by big banks - involving arms-length lending approaches and centralized organizational structures - could have a comparative advantage (Oxford Handbook, 2010a).

(viii) A large number of small banks put pressure on the supervisory resources of the central bank.

(ix) Small banks are potentially vulnerable to sector concentration risk. For instance, community banks in the US suffered losses due to their excessive reliance on lending to commercial real estate.

(x) Small banks are vulnerable to geographic concentration risk from the local economy.

(xi) Small banks are not big enough to finance big investments, including infrastructure.

(xii) Small banks are prone to local influence capture.

(xiii) A large number of small banks put pressure on the supervisory resources of the central bank.

### Payment Banks in India:

A Payments Bank is like any other bank, but operating on a small scale without involving any credit risk. In simple words, it can carry out most of the banking operations but can't give loans and can't issue credit cards. Payments Bank can accept demand deposits up to 1 lakh from individual customer, offer remmitance services, mobile payments/ transfers/purchases and other banking services like ATM/debit cards, net banking and third party fund transfers. A Payments bank is a new category of banks conceptualized by the Reserve Bank of India. Payments banks are smaller versions of Traditional Banks. Their objective is to reach low income house holds and small businesses through mobile phones rather than traditional offices. Besides, it can also act as a business correspondent for another bank.

Payment banks established with an aim to provide banking services to unbanked areas, mostly rural areas. Reserve Bank of India issued guidelines to setup Payments Banks. On 19$^{th}$ August 2015, the Reserve Bank of India gave "in-principle" licences to eleven entities to launch Payments Banks under Section 22(1) of the Banking Regulation Act, 1949. They are: Aditya Birla Nuvo (Aditya Birla Idea Payments Bank), Airtel M Commerce Services (Airtel Payments Bank Limited), Department of Posts (India Post Payments Bank), FINO PayTech, National Securities Depository, Reliance Industries (Jio Payments Bank), Paytm payments Bank, Vodafone M-Pesa, Google Pay, Phone Pay etc.

### Guidelines by RBI for Payment Banks

- These banks can able to operate current accounts and saving accounts. They can issue ATM or Debit cards, Net Banking and Mobile Banking facilities to their customers.
- The Payment Banks can take restricted deposits which is currently limited to 1 lakh per customer.
- They can distribute the non-risk financial products such as mutual funds and insurance.

### Restrictions on Payment Banks:

- They don't have rights to provide lending services such as credit cards and issue loan facilities.
- The initial minimum capital requirement of ₹ 100 crore is mandatory. 74% FDI is allowed.
- The promoter's contribution must be 40% for the first 5 years.

- Non-resident Indians (NRI) will not be allowed to open accounts in payment banks.
- They can be integrated with your savings bank accounts via IMPS and NEFT transfers and could enable transfers and remittances through a mobile phone.
- Payment Banks must maintain CRR minimum 75% of demand deposits in government bonds of upto one year.
- They must maintain maximum 25% in current and fixed deposits with other scheduled commercial banks for operational purpose and liquidity management.
- 25% of its branches must be in the unbanked rural area. The bank must use the term "payment bank" in its name to differentiate it from other types of bank.
- The banks will be licensed as Payments Banks under Section 22 of the Banking Regulation Act, 1949, and will be registered as public limited company under the Companies Act, 2013.
- The voting rights will be regulated by the Banking Regulation Act, 1949. The voting right of any shareholder is capped at 10% now.

## 2.2 BANK ACCOUNTS : TYPES, PROCEDURE AND OPERATION OF ACCOUNTS

### 2.2.1 Types of Bank Accounts

Acceptance of deposits and maintenance of accounts is the chief function of banks. The banks are free to devise deposit product within the guidelines framed by the Reserve Bank of India. The banks are also bound to follow the instructions on customer service issued by RBI from time to time. There are various types of deposit products offered by banks that are almost similar in nature however, with different assigned names.

**1. Saving Deposit**

Savings deposit accounts are accounts for primarily saving purpose which provides interest on deposit. However, the rate of interest differs from bank to bank as banks are free to decide the rate of interest. A saving deposit account can be opened in a single name or jointly in the names of two persons or more persons. Cash withdrawal is allowed by cheque or through a withdrawal slip accompanied by the passbook however the total number of withdrawals is restricted. A minimum amount of balance has to be maintained in a savings account, failing which service charges are levied including closure of account. There are two types of Savings Bank Accounts in India.

**1. Savings Account:**

Savings accounts are opened to encourage the people to save money and collect their savings. The account holder is allowed to withdraw money from the account as and when required. There is no restriction on the number and amount of deposits. However, in India, mandatory PAN details are required to be furnished for doing cash transactions exceeding ₹ 50,000. But withdrawals are allowed subject to certain restrictions. A minimum amount has to be kept on savings account to keep it functioning. Moreover, if you want cheque book then bank will provide also.

**(a) Basic Savings Bank Deposit Accounts (BSBDA):** This account will be considered as normal banking service. For this account, maintenance of minimum balance is not required. ATM card/ATM cum Debit card, Rupay card will be given for the account holders. There are going to be no limits on the number of deposits that can be made in a month but, account holders will be allowed at the most 4 withdrawals in a month, which includes ATM withdrawals also. The above facilities will be given without any charge. There will be no charge levied for non-operation/ activation of in-operative basic savings bank deposit account. For this account, overdraft facility will be provided up to ₹ 5,000/-.

**(b) Basic Savings Bank Deposit Accounts Small Scheme (BSBDS):** These are accounts with relaxed KYC, with a minimum document requirement of self-attested address proof and photograph. Total credit should not exceed 1 Lakh rupees in a year. Maximum balance should not exceed ₹ 50,000/- at any time. Cash withdrawals and transfers must not exceed ₹ 10,000/- in a month. Remittance from foreign account cannot be credited to this account without completing normal KYC formalities. This account can be opened only at Core Banking Solution linked branches of banks or at such branches, where it is possible to manually monitor the fulfillments of the conditions.

**2. Regular Savings Bank Account:**

Any resident individual-single accounts, two or more individuals in joint accounts, Associations, clubs, etc, are eligible for this account. A modest credit option is available to the depositor, Two free cheque books will be issued per year, Internet banking facility will be provided without any charge, Balance enquiry, NEFT, Bill payment, Mobile recharge etc., are provided through mobile phones, Students can open this account with zero balance by providing the required documents.

**Benefits of Savings Deposits Accounts:**

1. It is the simplest deposit option available to park surplus money.
2. Savings deposit accounts are easy to operate as money can be deposited from any bank branch or can be transferred online.
3. Money can be easily withdrawn through cheque, withdrawal slip or through ATM cum debit cards.
4. Savings deposit accounts offer cheque facility with certain number of free checkes annually.
5. The account holder can give standing instructions for transfer of funds from the account to another account.
6. Certain banks offer additional benefits with saving deposits account like personal accident insurance at low premium.

**3. Current Accounts**

Current Accounts are deposit accounts which allow withdrawal any number of times which are generally meant for the business community to conduct their business transactions smoothly. An account can be opened in individual name or jointly in the names of two or more persons.

- Accounts can be opened in the name of sole proprietor firms, private limited company, public limited company, joint Hindu family, trusts, clubs, associates, two or more individuals in joint accounts, Associations, Religious Institutions, Educational Institutions, Charitable Institutions, clubs, etc. are eligible for this account.
- Cheque book facility is provided and the account holder can deposit all types of the cheques and drafts endorsed in their favour by third parties.
- Payments can be done unlimited number of times.
- Usually bank do not pay any interest on such current accounts.
- These accounts do not have any fixed maturity as these are on continuous basis accounts.
- Funds can be remitted from any part of the country to the corresponding account.
- Overdraft facility will be available.
- Internet banking facility is available.

**4. Fixed Deposit Account:**

The account which is opened for a particular fixed period by depositing particular amount is known as Fixed Deposit (FD). The deposit can be withdrawn only after the specific period over. The minimum term for a term deposit can be seven days. RBI has given free hand to commercial banks to decide interest rate on domestic term deposit of various maturities. In case of premature withdrawal of a term deposit i.e. before completion of the period of term deposit, premature withdrawal is allowed with penalty. Moreover, banks give interest but only for specific days. Loan or overdraft facility is provided by bank against term deposit. The main purpose of FD account is to enable the individuals to earn a higher rate of interest on their surplus funds. The amount can be deposited only once. For further deposits, separate accounts need to be opened.

**(a) Short Deposit Receipt**

(a) Banks accept deposits from customers varying from 7 days to a maximum of 10 years.

(b) The period of 7 days and above but not exceeding 179 days deposits is classified as 'Short Deposits'.

(c) The minimum amount that can be deposited under this scheme is ₹ 5 lakh for a period of 7-14 days.

**(b) Fixed Deposit Receipt:**

- Any resident individual - single account, two or more individuals in joint accounts, associations, minors, societies, clubs, etc. are eligible for this account.
- The minimum FDR in metro and urban branches is ₹ 10,000/- and in rural and semi urban and for senior citizens it is ₹ 5,000/- .
- For the subsidy kept under the government sponsored schemes, margin money, earnest money and court attached/ordered deposits, minimum amount criteria will not be applicable.
- Depositors may ask for repayment of their deposits before maturity. Repayment of amount before maturity is allowable.
- Interest rate differs from bank to bank depending upon the tenure of the deposits and as and when the bank changes the interest rate.
- Additional interest of 0.50% is offered for senior citizens on deposits placed for a year and above.

**2. Recurring Deposit Account:**

Recurring account is a kind of term deposit where customer deposits a fixed sum on a regular basis. An individual, firm, partner and company, trust and societies are eligible to open a recurring account. The minimum amount and minimum term differs from bank to bank. The installment is to be paid on or before the last working day of that calendar month or else penalty is levied. In RD accounts, the maturity sum along with interest is paid at the end of the term. Generally premature withdrawal is allowed and loan or overdraft is provided against RD account.

- Any resident individual - single account, two or more individuals in joint accounts, associations, clubs, institutions/agencies specifically permitted by the RBI, etc. are eligible to open this account in single/joint names.
- Periodic/monthly instalments can be made for any amount starting from as low as ₹ 50/-.
- Account can be opened for any period ranging from 6 months to 120 months, in multiple of 1 month.
- The amount selected for installment at the start of the scheme will be payable every month.
- The number of installments once fixed, cannot be altered.
- Approved rate of interest is compounded every quarter.
- The amount after maturity will be paid to customers one month after the deposit of the last installment.
- Pass book will be given to the depositor.

TDS will be applicable on the interest, as per the latest changes in the Income Tax Act on cumulative deposits also.

**3. Demat Account:**

- Used to conduct stress-free transactions on the shares.
- An individual, Non-Resident Indian, Foreign Institutional Investor, Foreign National, Corporate, Trusts, Clearing Houses, Financial Institution, Clearing Member, Mutual Funds, Banks and Other Depository Account.
- For opening this account, an individual has to fill a form, submit a photo of the applicant along with a photocopy of Voter ID/ Passport/ Aadhar card/ Driving License and Demat account number will be provided to the applicant immediately after the completion of processing of the application.
- Facilities provided under this account are- Opening and maintaining of Demat accounts, Dematerialization, Rematerialization, Purchases, Sales, Pledging and Unpledging, safe custody.

## 2.2.2 Bank Accounts Procedure

For opening different types of accounts, different formalities are laid down and have got to be observed by the bankers as well as the customers. Let us go into details of these formalities.

### [A] Opening of Current and Savings Accounts

When a account is opened, a customer enters into relationship with the banker involving several obligations on the banker. Therefore, a banker must be careful in opening an account in the name of customer. The following formalities need be completed while opening a current or a saving bank account:

**(1) Know Your Customer (KYC) Needs and Norms:** Banks are required to provide a choice of a 'no frills account' where the minimum balance is nil or very small but having restrictions on number of withdrawals, etc., to facilitate easy access to bank accounts.

For the purpose of safety of funds - both from the bank's and customer's point of view 'Know Your Customer' norms are evolved. A KYC form contains details such as address, occupation, annual income, PAN Card No. etc. duly supported by specified proofs plus a photograph of the person who desires to open an account.

Further, in order to ensure that persons belonging to low income group both in urban and rural areas do not face difficulty in opening the bank accounts due to the procedural hassles, the 'KYC' procedure for opening accounts for those persons who intend to keep balances not exceeding rupees fifty thousand (₹ 50,000/-) in all their accounts taken together and the total credit in all the accounts taken together is not expected to exceed rupees one lakh (₹ 1,00,000/-) in a year has been simplified to enable those belonging to low income groups without documents of identity and proof of residence to open banks accounts. In such cases banks can take introduction from an account holder on whom full KYC procedure has been completed and has had satisfactory transactions with the bank for at least six months. Photograph of the customer who proposes to open the account and his address need to be certified by the introducer.

**Ensuring Reasonableness of Bank Charges**

As the Reserve Bank has been receiving several representations from public about unreasonable service charges being levied by banks, the existing institutional mechanism in this regard is not adequate. Accordingly, and in order to ensure fair practices in banking services, the

RBI has issued instructions to banks making it obligatory for them to display and continue to keep updated, in their offices/branches as also in their website, the details of various services charges in a format prescribed by it. The Reserve Bank has also decided to place details relating to service charges of individual banks for the most common services in its website.

**(2) Application Form:** A customer can request the concerned bank for opening an account, current or savings in his name by making an application in a form prescribed by the bank. Generally, different forms are used for savings and current account and also for individuals, partnership firms and joint-stock companies. The applicant is required to furnish all the relevant information in the application like his name, occupation, full address, specimen signature/s and the name and signature of a referee. He also undertakes to comply with the banks rules inforced for the conduct of the account.

**(3) Introduction of the Applicant (Introduction):** Since the banker reserves the right not to open an account in the name of a person whose true identity has not been established or who is considered to be an undesirable person, the banker has to get the true identity of the applicant properly established. The applicant can be introduced to the banker in any one of the three ways:

(a) A respectable person, i.e. a person who is a customer of the same branch or who is known to the staff of the branch, introduces him by signing his own name and address on the potential customers application form,

(b) The applicant may give the name of any respectable person or that of another bank as a referee. The banker may make a reference to the referee and find out whether the potential customer is respectable one. If no reply or adverse reply is sent by the referee, banker can refuse to open the account in his name,

(c) The R.B.I. has advised the banks to accept identity cards of people working in different departments or passports to consider sufficient for establishing identity of a person for opening an account without facility of cheques. It is necessary that, (i) The person recommending a potential customer is himself a respectable person, and (ii) That he knows the potential customer for a period long enough, so that he can vouch-safe the integrity and honesty of the potential customer.

**(4) Proof of Residence:** The bank asked the prospective account holder to give his proof of residence either by submitting his Election Voting Card and/or PAN Card and/or 'Adhar Card'.

**(5) Specimen Signature:** The customer applying for opening an account is required to furnish his specimen signatures, generally on a card for the purpose of the bankers record. These cards are preserved by the bank. Whenever the account-holder withdraws money from his accounts or issue cheques, the banker is expected to compare the signature with the specimen signature so as to detect any fraud or forgery.

**Importance of Introduction, Proof of Residence and Specimen Signature:**

(a) It avoids the frauds of various types in the operation of accounts.

(b) The banker is in a better position to answer queries from other bankers about the customer.

**(6) Nomination:** The Banking Laws (Amendment) Act, 1983 provides for the facility of nomination by depositors in bank.

(a) A depositor may nominate in prescribed manner, a person to whom the amount to his credit may be paid by the banker in the event of the depositor's death.

(b) All the depositors of a joint account can together nominate a person to whom the amount may be paid by the bank in the event of the death of all.

(c) Nomination can be made in favour of individuals only and not associations, trustees, or societies.

(d) Facility of nomination is available to all types of deposit accounts.

(e) A depositor may appoint any person to accept the amount due to the nominee if the latter is a minor.

(f) The nomination can be varied or cancelled by the depositor in a prescribed manner.

**Legal Status of the Nominee**

The legal status of the nominee had come up for discussion because of the question, Does the nominee become absolute owner of such amount or the claims of other legal heirs of the deceased remain unaffected by such nomination? According to a supreme court decision a mear nomination does not have the effect of conferring on the nominee, any beneficial interest in the amount payable. This decision was pertaining to Life Insurance Policy.

In the opinion of the court, the nomination only indicates the hand which is authorised to receive the amount, or the payment of which the insurer gets a valid discharge of its liability. The amount, however, can be claimed by the heirs, in accordance with the law of succession. Thus, it is clear that in spite of nomination the nominee does not become the absolute owner and the law of succession still prevails in deciding upon the claims of other legal heirs.

**Importance of Nomination:**

The nominees shall become entitled to all the rights of the depositor on the death, to the exclusion of all other persons unless the nomination has been varied or cancelled.

**(7) Opening the Account:** After all the formalities mentioned above are over, the banker opens an account in the name of the applicant. According to a decision of Indian Banks Association, the minimum initial deposit for opening a current account would be ₹ 1,000/- for Urban and ₹ 500/- for Rural branches. After opening of the account, the banker provides the customer with a deposit slip book, a cheque book and a pass book.

**SPECIMEN FORM OF OPENING AN ACCOUNT**

NAME OF FIRST DEPOSITOR ________ A/C. NO. ________

**DENA BANK** ____________ BRANCH.

DATE ________

**Head Office:** 41, Budhwar Peth, PUNE.

SAVINGS BANK A/C.

I/We hereby request you to open in your bank a savings ACCOUNT in my/our name(s) which I/We deposit initially ₹ ________ (Rupees ______________________ only). I/We declare that Bank's Savings Rules have been read by me/us and I/We accept them as binding upon me / us

SPECIAL INSTRUCTIONS : ______________________________

ACCOUNT TO BE OPERATED BY AND
BALANCE PAYABLE TO

ME JOINTLY TO US Either/Anyone
of us/survivor(s)

☐ ☐ ☐ ☐

| NAME (SPECIMEN) | SIGNATURE(S) |
|---|---|
| | |
| | |
| | |

S.B.A/C. NO. __________ INSTRUCTION ____________

FIRST NAME ______________________________

ADDRESS ______________________________

Specimen Signature ______________________________

DATE ______________________________

| FULL NAME(S) (IN BLOCK LETTERS) | OCCUPATION |
|---|---|
| 1. | |
| 2. | |
| 3. | |
| 4. | |

ADDRESS (OF FIRST DEPOSITOR): ____________________

TELEPHONE: ____________

DATE OF BIRTH
(MINOR'S A/C. ONLY)

| NAME(S) OF NOMINEE(S) | RELATIONSHIP | AGE | REMARKS |
|---|---|---|---|
| | | | |
| | | | |

ADDRESS (OF FIRST NOMINEE): ____________

____________________

NOMINEE(S) DATE OF BIRTH (IF MINOR): ________

INTRODUCTION: "I Certify that I have known MR./MRS./MS.
____________ Since the past ________
months/years and confirm his/her occupation and address as stated in the application.

| | |
|---|---|
| INTRODUCER'S NAME: | |
| ACCOUNT NO: | |
| BRANCH | INTRODUCER'S SIGNATURE |
| VERIFIED | |
| AUTHORISED SIGNATORY | DATE ACCOUNT OPENED |

**[B] Opening of Fixed Deposit Accounts**

For opening a fixed deposit account, a depositor is required to fill in an application form. In this form he mentions the amount of the deposits and the period for which he desires to keep the deposit with the bank. He also gives his specimen signature. A fixed deposit receipt is thereafter issued to the depositor, acknowledging the receipt of the amount. The fixed deposit receipt also specifies the interest rate payable on the deposit and the date on which the deposit would mature. The rules regarding the maturity of the deposit, the time of paying interest, the procedure to claim refund etc. are sometimes printed on the backside of the deposit receipt.

Fixed deposits are usually made with the bank in the joint names of two or more persons payable to either of them or survivor. Such deposit is a joint debt owned by a bank to the depositors. In accordance with the terms of the receipts, it is payable to either of them or survivor.

## 2.3 RECENT TRENDS IN INDIAN BANKING ENVIRONMENT

### 2.3.1 E-Banking

Banking system has an important role to play in every country's economy. It is vital for any nation as it provides the needs of credit for all the sections of the society. Banking in India has been a long journey. It has seen a number of changes due to technology and innovation. Arrival of card, introduction of Electronic Clearing Service (ECS) introduction of Electronic Funds Transfer and concept of online banking and mobile banking are the various novelties which took place in banking sector. Now all the banks have started with the concept of multi- channels, like ATMs, credit cards, debit cards, telephone/mobile banking, internet banking, etc. The role of banking has now changed from a mere financial intermediary to service provider of various financial services under one roof acting like a financial supermarket. With extreme competition among the banks, entire banking system is undergoing a change. Today, modern banking not only looks for new ways to attract but also to retain the customers and gain competitive advantage over their competitors. As the name implies, electronic banking or e-banking involves combination of electronic technology with the banking sector. It relates to provision of banking products and services through electronic delivery channel. Under this system, the banking services are delivered by way of a computer controlled system. e-banking involves providing banking and related services through extensive use of information technology without direct recourse to the bank by the customer. With growing popularity and benefits of e-banking, lots of banks have realized the importance, competition and challenges brought forth with this new technology and are adapting to this new-age banking.

**Definition of E-Banking:**

**Daniel (1999)** defines *electronic banking as "the delivery of bank's information and services by banks to customers via different delivery platforms that can be used with different terminal devices such as a personal computer and a mobile phone with browser or desktop software, telephone or digital television".*

**Barron's Dictionary (2006)** *"As a form of banking where funds are transferred through an exchange of electronic signals between financial institutions, rather than an exchange of cash, checks or other negotiable instruments".*

Internet banking (e-banking) facilitates customers to avail various small and large value banking products and services through electronic channels. Internet banking comprises banking activities or services which can be availed by the customers at any point of time and from any places with their convenience, it is also called PC banking, online banking, cyber banking, virtual banking, etc. Internet banking delivers banking services through the open access computer network i.e. internet, directly to customers' home that can be used with different electronic devices such as personal computer, mobile phone with a browser or desktop software, digital television. So, we can say that Internet Banking is about using banking facilities via the internet with the help various electronic devices.

**Features of e-Banking:**

(i) Easy Electronic Fund Transfer facility

(ii) Better efficiency in Customer Relationship Management

(iii) Making the Payments of bills like electricity, telephone bills and mobile recharge

(iv) It introduces virgin and innovative banking products and services

(v) It can view of balance of accounts and statements

(vi) E-banking can bring doorstep services

(vii) Balance and transaction history search

(viii) Transaction history export

(ix) Order mini statements

(x) Mobile banking

(xi) Pay anyone payments multi payments

(xii) SMS banking services

**Sources/Services of e-Banking:**

(i) Automated Teller Machines (ATM)

(ii) Credit Cards

(iii) Debit Cards

(iv) Smart Cards

(v) Electronic Funds Transfer (EFT) System,

(vi) Mobile Banking

(vii) Internet Banking

(viii) Telephone banking

(ix) Electronic Clearing Services

**Current Scenario of E-Banking in India:**

Internet Banking has become an integral part of the banking system in India. The concept of e-banking is of fairly recent origin in India. Till the early 90's, traditional model of banking i.e. branch-based banking was prevalent, but after that non-branch banking services was started. The Indian government enacted the IT Act, 2000, with effect from 17th October, 2000. To examine different aspects of Internet banking RBI set up a committee on Internet Banking. The committee had focused on three major areas of Internet Banking, technology and security issues, legal issues and regulatory and supervisory issues. RBI had accepted the suggestions and recommendations of the working committee and accordingly issued guidelines to banks to implement internet banking in India. The old manual systems which were prevalent in Indian banking for centuries seem to replaced by modern technologies. Following table exhibits a few facts and figures related to internet/electronic banking to present its current scenario. It shows evidence for ATM, POS (Point of Sale) and electronic cards (credit and debit cards) deployed in India as on March, 2016. Table 2.3 compares the data of March, 2016 with March, 2012. It shows growth rate of these banking channels and it seems to be great in Indian context.

**Table 2.3: Number of E-channels**

| Types of Electronic Channels | Year | | | Growth in % (2012-2016) |
|---|---|---|---|---|
| | 2012 | 2016 | 2018 | |
| Number of ATMs deployed | 95686 | 199099 | 207920 (0.05)* | 108.07 |
| Number of POS deployed | 660920 | 1385668 | - | 109.65 |
| Number of Credit Cards issued | 17653818 | 24505219 | 37782876 (24.39)* | 38.81 |
| Number of Debit Card issued | 278282839 | 661824092 | 906356781 (16.08)* | 227.82 |
| Number of NEFT (in million) | - | - | 1946.36 | 20.00* |
| Number of RTGS (in million) | - | - | 124.46 | 15.39* |

**Source:** International Journal of Science and Research (IJSR), Volume 5 Issue 12, December 2016 and Journal of Management Research and Analysis, October-December, 2018.

**Note:** *Shows 2017 to 2018 growth in %.

From the above table, it is clearly shown that no doubt Indian banks are making sincere efforts for the adoption of advanced technology and installation of e-delivery channels but still the concept and scope of e-banking is still evolving. It facilitates an effective payment and accounting system thereby enhancing the speed of delivery of banking services considerably. While e-banking has improved efficiency and convenience, it has also posed several challenges to the regulators and supervisors. Several initiatives taken by the government of India, as well as the Reserve Bank of India (RBI), have facilitated the development of e-banking in India.

From the above table, it is clearly shown that no doubt Indian banks are making sincere efforts for the adoption of advanced technology and installation of e-delivery channels but still the concept and scope of e-banking is still evolving. It facilitates an effective payment and accounting system thereby enhancing the speed of delivery of banking services considerably. While e-banking has improved efficiency and convenience, it has also posed several challenges to the regulators and supervisors. Several initiatives taken by the Government of India, as well as the Reserve Bank of India (RBI), have facilitated the development of e-banking in India. As already discussed, the Government of India enacted the IT Act, 2000 which provides legal recognition to electronic transactions and other means of electronic commerce. The RBI has been preparing to upgrade itself as a regulator and supervisor of the technologically dominated financial system. It issued guidelines on risks and control in computer and telecommunication system to all banks, advising them to evaluate the risks inherent in the systems and put in place adequate control mechanisms to address these risks. The existing regulatory framework over banks has also been extended to e-banking. It covers various issues that fall within the framework of technology, security standards and legal and regulatory issues.

**Functions of E-Banking:**

The personal e-banking system provides the following services:

**(i)** **Inquire About Information of Account:** The client inquires about the details of his own account information such as the card's/account's balance and the detailed historical records of the account and downloads the report list.

**(ii)** **Card accounts transfer:** The client can transfer the fund to another person's Credit Card on the same city.

(iii) **Bank-securities account transfer:** The client can achieve the fund transfer between his own bank savings accounts of his own Credit Card account and his own capital account in the securities company. Moreover, the client can inquire about the present balance at real time.

(iv) **Foreign exchange transaction:** The client can do the real-time transfer and get the feedback information about payment from own bank when the client does shopping in the appointed website.

(v) **Client Service:** The client can modify the login password, information of the Credit Card and the client information in e-bank on net.

(vi) **Account Management:** The client can modify his own limits of right and state of the registered account in the personal e-bank, such as modifying his own login password, freezing or deleting some cards and so on.

(vii) **Reporting the loss, if any:** The client can report the loss in the local area (not nationwide) when the client's Credit Card or passbook is missing or stolen.

**Advantages of e-banking:**

**A. For Costumers**

(i) **Less Waiting Time:** It offers less waiting time and more convenience as compared to the traditional banking system and significantly lowers the cost structure than traditional delivery channels. It also reduces the time and place limitation and it provides various benefits to consumers so that they feel convenient while doing banking activities.

(ii) **Ease and Convenience:** Internet Banking is considered as more efficient in terms of ease of use and access. It allows the consumers to make transactions on internet by providing them comfort of home or office without going outside. It also enables consumers to keep an eye on their transactions or account activities from their home, office or elsewhere so they can feel satisfied and convenient. Even non transactional facilities like ordering check books online, updating accounts, inquiring about interest rates of various financial products, etc. have become much simpler on the internet.

**(iii) 24×7 Availability:** With the help of internet banking, costumers can access their banking facilities and services all around the clock i.e. 24 hours and 365 days from anywhere, anytime. They don't need to wait for timing of bank branches.

**(iv) Self Service Channel:** Internet Banking provides their customers a self service channel for various banking services. They do have not to depend on the bank's staff and other depending process to avail their services. Internet Banking is one of the most popular self-service banking technologies. Continued use of self service technology has positively affected by buyers' perceived usefulness.

**(v) Save Time and Money:** Now customers don't have to go to branch to avail banking services. It consist various advantages such as: it will save time, save fuel, do away from traffic, save the environment in terms of reducing the use of motor vehicles and reduce waiting time.

**B. For Banks:**

**(i) Increased Profitability:** Adoption of internet helps the banks to increase their profitability. Banks with Internet Banking have better operating efficiency ratios and profitability as compared to banks which are not using internet facilities. The banks can provide banking services to the consumers using internet banking at a far lower cost as compared to the traditional banking.

**(ii) Cost Effective Mechanism:** The internet banking provides an opportunity of self service channel to the consumers. This helps the banks to cut their workforce up to a particular extent that results in reducing the administrative costs borne by the banks. Compared to traditional banking system, internet banking is cost-effective as it reduces the administrative costs and paperwork needed for the bank transactions. Many studies show that electronic banking has successfully reduced operating and administrative costs and fees.

**(iii) Reach Where There is no branch:** Internet banking has expanded it's geographical reach and may increase customer base by deploying electronic delivery channels at lower a cost. Actually, some banks are doing in that way. They are providing banking services exclusively via the internet in some areas because they do not have bank branches in these areas. whereas many financial institutions are using the internet banking as a branchless banking to satisfy their existing customers and attract new customers in the perspective of convenience and cost-effectiveness.

(iv) **Improve Customer Relationship:** Maintaining the relationship with consumers has become a strategic priority for most of the banks. Using the internet banking technology and facilities can provide a means for banks to develop and maintain a good relationship with their customers by offering easy access to a wide range of products and services. Managing a good relationship with the customers may help to increase customer loyalty, customer retention and improve cross-selling. Internet banking facilities have become a useful tool for improving customer satisfaction and increasing cross-selling opportunities.

(v) **Eco-Friendly Image:** Another important benefit of internet banking is that it is eco-friendly is nature. Internet banking cuts down the paper usage and reduces pollution as people do not have to travel physically and also does not add carbon emissions. Implementing the e-banking facilities in the banks show the concern of the bank towards the environment, which further, will help the banks to create an eco-friendly image.

**Challenges in adoption of E-banking:**

E-banking is facing following challenges in Indian banking industry:

(i) **Security risk:** The problem related to security has become one of the major concerns for banks. A large group of customers refuses to opt for e-banking facilities due to uncertainty and security concerns. According to the IAMAI Report (2006), 43% of internet users are not using internet banking in India because of security concerns. So it's a big challenge for marketers to makes consumers satisfied regarding their security concerns, which may further increase the online banking use.

(ii) **Privacy risk:** The risk of disclosing private information and fear of identity theft is one of the major factors that inhibit the consumers while opting for internet banking services. Most of the consumers believe that using online banking services make them vulnerable to identity theft. According to the study, consumers' worry about their privacy and feel that bank may invade their privacy by utilizing their information for marketing and other secondary purposes without consent of consumers.

**(iii) The Trust Factor:** Trust is the biggest hurdle to online banking for most of the customers. Conventional banking is preferred by the customers because of lack of trust on the online security. They have a perception that online transaction is risky due to which frauds can take place. While using e-banking facilities lot of questions arises in the mind of customers such as: Did the transaction go through? Did I push the transfer button once or twice? Trust is among the significant factors which influence the customers' willingness to engage in a transaction with web merchants.

**(iv) Customer Awareness:** Awareness among customers about the e-banking facilities and procedures is still at lower side in Indian scenario. Banks are not able to disseminate proper information about the use, benefits and facility of internet banking. Less awareness of new technologies and their benefits is among one of the most top ranked barrier in the development of e-banking.

**(v) Less Internet Penetration in Indian Context**: The internet banking channel has evolved over the years. The knowledge and availability of internet is still a one of the biggest challenges that prevails in Indian context. According to the report of IAMAI 2006, around 22% of internet users do not have knowledge about transferring online. So the penetration of internet and knowledge related to internet are major hurdles.

**(vi) High Star-up Cost:** E-banking requires high initial start-up cost. It includes internet installation cost, cost of advanced hardware, software, modem, computers, cost of maintenance of all computer equipments and cost of reorganizational structure.

**(vii) Lack of Professionals:** There is shortage of web developers', content providers and knowledgeable professionals to perform banking activities through internet.

**(viii) Restricted Business:** All banking transactions cannot be performed electronically. Many banking activities require personal visit of customers.

**(ix) Competition:** The nationalized banks and commercial banks have competition from foreign and new private sector banks. Competition in banking sector brings various challenges before the banks such as product positioning, innovative ideas and channels, new market trends, cross selling etc. At managerial and organizational part, this system needs to be manage.

**Opportunities for E-Banking:**

Despite various challenges that are prevailing in context with e-banking in India, the following opportunities are motivating the marketers for implementing e-banking:

**(i) Increasing Internet Users and Computer Literacy:** To use internet banking, it is very important or initial requirement that people should have knowledge about internet technology so that they can easily adopt the internet banking services. The fast increasing internet users in India can be a very big opportunity and banking industry should encash this opportunity to attract more internet users to adopt internet banking services. Following Table 2.4 shows the evidence of increasing number of internet users in India. As per the last available data, as on 1 July 2014, there are 243, 198,922 Indians who are using internet and it is increasing approximately at the rate of 3.5 crores every year on an average. It is also shows the rate of growth which is 168 percent since 2010. It is very much evident through the data provided by IAMAI (The Internet and Mobile Association of India). According to the ComScore Report, 2013 India is now world's third largest Internet user after U.S. and China. The computer literacy has gone upward in the last decade. Those with higher IT literacy may have a more positive perception towards e-banking in general and may thus, be more likely to accept e-banking services.

**Table 2.4 : Internet Users in India**

| Years | 2010 | 2011 | 2012 | 2013 | 2014 |
|---|---|---|---|---|---|
| Internet Users | 90,421,849 | 122,970,441 | 441,155,575 | 213,339,324 | 243,198,922 |
| New Users | 29,486,779 | 32,548,593 | 32,605,503 | 57,763,380 | 29,859,598 |
| Average | | | 36,452,770 | | |
| Growth | 0% | 36% | 72% | 136% | 168% |

**Source:** Chauhan and Choudhary, Apeejay - Journal of Management Sciences and Technology 2 (3), June - 2015.

*As on July 1 of every year.

**(ii) Initiatives taken by government agencies for financial literacy:** Financial literacy and education play a crucial role in financial inclusion and inclusive growth. A study reported that there is significant impact of financial literacy on use of internet banking. If customers are not financially educated they will simply avoid using new online services and not change their traditional way of banking. Thus, banks will not be able to convert users into their new online banking strategies. Various government institutions like RBI, SEBI, IRDA and various other market players have taken a number of initiatives on financial education. They have prepared a school curriculum along with various topics including internet banking, banking product and services, net banking to educate the school students, college students, working executives, middle income group, home makers, retired personnel, self help groups, etc.

**(iii) Competitive Advantage:** The benefit of adopting e-banking provides a competitive advantage to the banks over other players. The implementation of e-banking is beneficial for banks in many ways as it reduces cost to banks, improves customer relations, increases the geographical reach of the bank, etc. The benefits of e-banking have become opportunities for the banks to manage their banking business in a better way.

ICICI Bank initiated internet banking in India and later in the year 1999, HDFC Bank and Citibank followed the same. In today's scenario, with the help of internet, various banking and financial services are provided by banks in India. With the time, the concept of internet banking has got attention in the Indian context. Most of the banks have already implemented the e-banking facilities as these facilities are beneficial to both i.e. banks as well as consumers. But the adoption of e-banking by the consumers is still at the early stage due to various challenges. The challenges such as security risk, privacy risk, trust factor and less awareness among consumers about e-banking are acting as hurdles in the adoption of e-banking facilities. Considering the challenges and risks related to e-banking, the Government of India along with various government agencies is making an effort to make e-banking more safe, secure and reliable.

### 2.3.2 E-Wallets

Any modern economy develops based on the trade exchanges that involve the making of money payments. In fact, the payment represents a money transfer from a beneficiary to an assets or services seller. The origins of the payments can be found in the antique barter system, which represented a payment in kind through direct interchange of goods. Due to the reduced flexibility of this modality, there have been developed payments systems based on the fiduciary currency and more and more advanced systems.

In the modern world, the frequent forms of manifestation of the payments involve the money, the cheques and bank transfers and in case of the business processes such payments are usually preceded by an invoice or followed by a form of the receipt. At this moment, the industry of e-payments is focused on e-transfers based on card emulation and there are many successful implementations described. All of these systems are focused on card or bank account emulations and that means that the user has to connect with the bank to generate a money transfer. In fact, we propose a new vision for managing money in an e-wallet by using the Near Field Communication (NFC) technology and the network communications. NFC is a short distance wireless technology that normally requires a distance of 4-10 cm to initialize a connection between two mobile devices. It is a standard that extends RFID (Radio Frequency Identification) combining the interface between a smartcard and a reader in one device.

Virtual cash or Cashless Transaction is an upcoming technology that has seen a tremendous growth in the past year. Cashless payments are now becoming a popular trend in almost every field. Cashless services are proving to be the future of transaction services with minimum or no use of physical cash. It is also being considered an alternative to plastic cash.

**"An electronic wallet is a virtual or a cashless service used as a substitute for physical cash".**

There are some applications of virtual cash on the internet. Some of them are Paytm, Freecharge, Mobikwik. All these applications provide commodities like bill payments, DTH recharge, etc. Paytm also has its own online shopping portal where a registered user can shop and pay via the app itself. All these applications work on credit system. The user has to give his credit card number once and then his account is linked to the app. So whenever he makes a transaction, the app automatically sends a request to the respective bank for credit payment. Millions of people have found these apps to be very useful and efficient. It saves a lot of time when we use these apps instead of physical or plastic cash. The user has to only use plastic cash once while registration.

**Characteristics of E-Wallet:**

1. **Atomicity:** This characteristic takes into account that during the transfer no existing money is lost or no money is created.
2. **The impossibility of the Non-Reputation:** None of the users involved in the transaction can decline their responsibility conferred by the electronic signature.

3. **Security:** The system must retain the possibility of frauds within the electronic environment.
4. **Availability:** The systems must be accessible and available at any moment of time.
5. **Cost efficiency:** The transaction cost must be reasonable even in the case of micro-payments.
6. **Integration and scalability:** The systems must be inter-operable with all the other existing systems. They must also integrate themselves with the new payment methods from the online environment.
7. **The Ease of Using:** Any system of electronic payments must be accessible through different types of hardware terminals and from different software platforms.
8. **Confidentiality:** The data regarding the parties involved in the transactions must be available for the others only up to the confidentiality level established by the collaboration protocol.

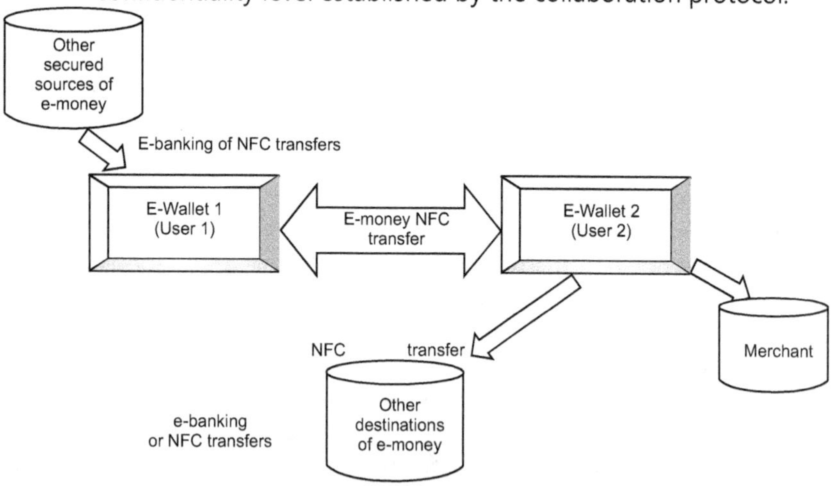


**Fig. 2.2: New Architecture for E-Wallet**

Seen in the Fig. 2.2, is the e-money transfer between User1 and User2, supposing that both users have smart devices with Near Field Communication (NFC) capabilities included. The money is stored in a secured application and it is transferred through the NFC tags. The application is developed on Android platform and uses NDF Data Exchange Format (NDEF) in order to transfer the messages between devices. Every message includes secured information about:

- The amount of transferred money

- The security certificate of every monetary unit (because in our model, every monetary unit has its own security certificate)
- The payer
- The receiver
- The date of the transfer

**Benefits of E-Wallet:**

1. Send and receive payments anywhere in the world
2. Unlimited transfers
3. Easy recurring payments and transfer
4. Manage our account from our mobile phone
5. World Ventures-branded prepaid MasterCard available
6. Security for our bank account and credit card numbers
7. Email or SMS notifications after transactions
8. We are in complete control
9. Access our commissions faster
10. Pull money into our e-wallet from any bank account
11. Receive wired funds/transfers directly into our e-wallet
12. Any bank account worldwide
13. Transfer money from e-wallet to e-wallet without sharing personal account numbers
14. Request paper commissions checks

**Issues of E-Wallet:**

Main issue that should be taken care of for electronic payments system is Authentication which identifies buyer and also makes sure that person is the one who he/she claims to be. Used methods are i.e. digital signature, finger prints, password or smartcards, etc. Data integrity which means, that there must be a way to verify that data is not changed during the transactions. Confidentially must also be preserved.

### 2.3.3 Bank Mergers and Amalgamations

Mergers in Banking Sector in India have initially taken place to strengthen the banking system by merging the weak/loss making and inefficient banks with other profit making and strong banks. But in recent times, some mergers have taken place between profit making banks for availing the benefits by way of synergies to mergers. Indian Banking system has witnessed several mergers that have taken place for various reasons over a period of time.

**Meaning of Mergers and Amalgamations:**

Merger can be defined as a means of unification of two players into single entity. Merger is a process of combining two business entities under the common ownership. Bank merger is an event when previously distinct banks are consolidated into one institution. A merger occurs when an independent bank loses its charter and becomes a part of an existing bank with one headquarter and a unified branch network.

**Purpose of Mergers and Amalgamations:**

The basic purpose of merging the company is to achieve faster growth in the corporate world. Faster growth of the company may be shelf through product improvement and other purposes for amalgamation are given below:

(i) **Procurement of Supplies:** The company by the way of merging and amalgamations can safeguard the sources of supplies of raw materials and obtain economies of purchase in the form of discount, saving cost of transportation costs, overhead costs in buying department, etc. The companies get merged to achieve this purpose.

(ii) **Revamping Production Facilities:** To achieve the economies of large scale by amalgamating production facilities is more intensive utilisation of plant and resources.

To obtain improved production technology and knowhow from the offered company.

(iii) **Market Expansion and Strategy:** To eliminate competition and protect existing market. To reduce the cost of advertising and to improve the public image of the offeree.

(iv) **Financial Strength:** To improve the liquidity and have direct access to the cash resources. To utilise the tax benefits. To dispose of surplus and outdated assets for cash out of combined companies.

(v) **General Gain:** The company is said to improve its own image and attract superior managerial talents to manage its affairs by the way of merger and amalgamation. The most general purpose of merging is to offer better satisfaction of product to the consumers or uses of the product.

(vi) **Strategic Purpose:** The company view the merger to achieve strategic objectives through different types of combinations which may be horizontal, vertical, product expansions other specific unrelated objectives depending upon the corporate strategies. Thus, these types of combinations are distinct from each other in their nature and are adopted to pursue the objectives.

(vii) **Corporate friendliness:** Although its rare but its true that business homes exhibit degrees of cooperative spirit despite fight in providing rescue to each completely different from hostile takeovers and cultivate things of collaboration sharing goodwill of each to realize performance heights through business combination. The corporate aim at circular combos by following this objective.

**Procedure of Banks Merger and Acquisition:**

1. The procedure for merger either voluntary or otherwise is printed within the several state statutes/the banking rules act, The registrars, being the authorities, United Nations agency are unconditional with the responsibility of administering the provisions are going to be guaranteeing that the due process of law prescribed within the statutes been complied with before they look for the approval of the run.
2. While choosing the merger, the approved officers of the exploit bank and therefore the merging bank sits on and it discuss concerning the procedural modalities and financial terms. Once the discussion is finished, a theme is ready to include all the small prints of each the banks and therefore the space terms and conditions. Once the theme is finalised, its been tabled among the meeting of board of administrators of banks. The board discusses concerning the theme and accords its confirmation if the proposal is found to be financially viable and useful at the end of the day.
3. After the board approval of the merger proposal, an additional normal general meeting of the shareholders of the several banks is converned to debate the proposal and look for their approval.
4. After the board approval of the merger proposal, a registered appraiser is appointed to evaluate each the banks. The appraiser valuates the banks on the premise of its share capital, market capital, assets and liabilities, it's reach and anticipated growth and seeks their approval.
5. Once the valuation is accepted by the several banks, they send the proposal besides all relevant documents like board approval, shareholders approval, valuation report, etc to Reserve Bank of India and alternative restrictive bodies such Security and Exchange Board of India for his or her approval.

6. At last when getting approvals from all the establishments, approved officers of each the banks they sit along to debate and settle share allocation proportion by the exploit bank to the shareholders of the merging bank.
7. After finishing higher than procedures then it'll be signed by the banks.

**Types of Mergers and Acquisitions:**

**Vertical Merger:**

VM is a merger in which one firm supplies it's products to the other. A vertical merger results in the consolidation of firms that have actual or potential buyer-seller relationships.

**Horizontal Merger:**

HM is the merger of two or more companies operating in the same field and in the same stages of process of attaining the same commodity or service. In other words, a horizontal merger is the combination of firms that are direct rivals selling substitutable products within overlapping geographical markets.

**Conglomerate Merger:**

CM occurs when unrelated enterprises combine or firms which compete in different product markets and which are situated at different production stages of the same or similar products combine to enter into different activity fields in the shortest possible time span and reduce financial risks by portfolio diversification.

**Concentric Merger:**

This involves firms which have different business operation patterns, though divergent, but may be highly related in production and distribution technologies. The acquired company represents an extension of the product lines, market participation or technologies of the acquiring firm under concentric M and A.

**Stages of Merger and Acquisition:**

A five-stage model that will result in successful pursuit of synergistic gains from M and A:

(a) Corporate strategy development
(b) Organizing for acquisitions
(c) Deal structuring and negotiation
(d) Post-acquisition integration and
(e) Post-acquisition audit and organizational learning

**(a) Corporate Strategy Development:** Corporate strategy development is concerned 'with ways of optimizing the portfolios of businesses that a firm currently owns and how this portfolio can be changed to serve the interests of the corporation's stakeholders.

**(b) Organizing for Acquisition:** The firm lays down the criteria for potential acquisitions consistent with the strategic objectives and value creation logic of the firm's corporate strategy and business model.

**(c) Deal Structuring and Negotiation:** This involves following stages of M and As:

(i) Valuing target companies, taking into account how the acquirer plans to leverage it's own assets with those of the target; choice of advisers to the deal;

(ii) Obtaining and evaluating as much intelligence as possible about the target from the target as well as other sources through due diligence;

(iii) Determining the range of negotiation parameters including the walk-away price negotiating warranties and indemnities; negotiating the positions of senior management of both firms in the post merger dispensation; and

(iv) Developing the appropriate bid and defense strategies and tactics within the parameters set by the relevant regulatory regimes.

**(d) Post-Acquisition Integration:** This stage involves the combination of the distinct organizations into one, resulting in changes in both the target and the acquirer, to deliver the strategic and value expectations that informed the merger.

**Provisions Relating to Merger, Acquisition and Amalgamation of Banks:**

**(i) Mergers-Banking Regulation Act, 1949:** Section 44A of this act talks about the procedures for voluntary mergers of banking companies. Section 45 of this act talks about the compulsory amalgamation of banks.

**(ii) Companies Act:** Section 230 and 232 of The Companies Act, 2013 relates with the mergers and amalgamations.

**(iii) State Bank of India, 1955:** Section 35 states acquisition of business of other banks by State Bank of India.

**Phases of Mergers in Banking Sector:**

To study the trends in mergers, the period from 1961 to 2017 is divided into various phases on the basis of time frame in line with the policy initiatives of the Government. The overall mergers in the banking sector and the trends are presented in the following tables. Phase wise mergers in Banking Sector in India are presented in Table 2.5.

**Table 2.5: Phases of Mergers in Banking Sector in India**

| Sr. No | Phase | Period | No. of Mergers |
|---|---|---|---|
| 1 | I - Pre-nationalisation | 1961 to 1969 | 46 |
| 2 | II - Post-nationalisation | 1969 to 1991 | 13 |
| 3 | III - Post-liberalisation | 1991 to 2015 | 22 |
| 4 | IV - Consolidation | 2015 and above | 5 |
| | | | Total 86 |

**Source:** SUMEDHA Journal of Management, Vol. 6, No. 4, Oct.-Dec. 2017

**Phase I - Pre-nationalisation Period (1961 - 1969):**

The above classification is made on the basis of the time frames during which various changes have taken place on account of Governmental Policy initiatives in the Banking Sector. The period before 1969 is considered as Pre-nationalisation period, during which several banks were operating in the Private Sector excepting for a few banks in the Public Sector. During this period, a major chunk of mergers i.e. 46 mergers have taken place. The major initiatives in the Banking Sector was the establishment of Reserve Bank of India in the year 1935 followed by the enactment of Banking Regulation Act in the year 1949. Nationalisation of Imperial Bank of India and renaming it as State Bank of India in the year 1955 which acted as the principal agent of RBI to handle the banking transactions of both the Central and State Governments; followed by nationalising the subsidiaries of SBI in the year 1959. During the first phase of prenationalisation, the growth was very slow and banks experienced periodic failures. People had less confidence in the banks because of which deposit mobilisation was also very slow. Reserve Bank of India (RBI) was vested with extensive powers for the supervision of banking in India as the Central Banking Authority. RBI formulated schemes for the reconstitution and compulsory merger of weak banks with the sound banks to strengthen the banking system.

The process of strengthening the banking structure through a process of merger and amalgamation of the weaker units with stronger institutions, following the failure of certain banks in 1960, continued during the year 1961. From the Table 2.5, it can be seen that in total, forty six bank mergers have taken place in India from the period between

1961 to 1968; out of which thirty mergers have taken place in the year 1961 itself; another ten mergers have taken place in the year 1964; three in the year 1965 and one each in the years of 1962, 1963 and 1968. The major reason for these mergers was the restructuring of weak banks in order to protect the customers' interests. Most of these mergers were between private banks.

**Phase II - Post-nationalisation Period (1969 - 1991):**

The period from 1969 to 1991 is Post-nationalisation Period. During this period, the Government of India has nationalised 14 commercial banks with total deposits of ₹ 50 crores in the year 1969, which gave Government a control over 84% of total branches; 6 banks with a total deposits of ₹ 200 crores were nationalised in the year 1980 which increased the total branch network of the nationalised banks to 91%. These banks were nationalised with the objectives to prevent few big business houses from controlling the banks; to prevent the concentration of economic power and maximisation of wealth in few hands; to mobilize savings from all sections of people throughout the country. The active participation of the nationalised banks in the mergers is seen during this phase.

During the post-nationalisation period, thirteen bank mergers have taken place from 1969 to 1990. All these mergers were between the Public Sector and Private Sector Banks. Out of these thirteen mergers, State Bank of India topped the list with three mergers to its credit during the years 1969; 1970 and again in the year 1985. Remaining ten mergers took place between the nationalised banks and other banks in the private sector. Year wise analysis of the mergers points to the fact that two out of fourteen mergers have taken place in the year 1969; one merger by State Bank of India and the other one was by New Bank of India (nationalised in the year 1980); again after a gap of fifteen years, three mergers have taken place with Union Bank of India; Canara Bank and State Bank of India; after a gap of five years in the year 1990, four mergers have taken place just before the liberalisation of economy.

**Phase III - Post-liberalisation Period (1991 - 2015):**

The period after 1991 is post-liberalisation period during which major economic reforms were initiated by the Government to revive Indian economy. In the year 1991, under the chairmanship of Mr. M Narasimham, a committee was constituted for strengthening the Banking Sector in India and to examine all aspects relating to the structure; organisation; functions and procedures of the financial system; These reforms were popularly known as 'structural adjustments' or liberalization' or 'globalization'. The Government announced a New Economic Policy on July 24, 1991. The new policy deregulated industrial economy in a substantial manner. One of the steps taken to liberalize and globalize Indian economy was the wide-ranging Financial Sector Reforms in the Banking, Capital Markets and Insurance Sectors, including the deregulation of interest rates, strong regulation and supervisory systems and the introduction of foreign/private sector competition. This period has witnessed the increased participation of Indian Private Sector Banks.

Total twenty two mergers have taken place during the post-liberalisation period from 1991 to 2015. One interesting merger that took place was between two nationalised banks Punjab National Bank and New Bank of India the reason being high Non-performing Assets. Thirteen mergers have taken place between Public Sector Banks and Private Sector Banks; eight mergers have taken place amongst the Private Sector Banks. Out of these twenty two, twelve mergers were forced mergers because of the financial sickness of the banks; eight have taken place voluntarily; and two were in the lines of consolidation.

**Phase IV: Consolidation of Banks (2015 and Above):**

The consolidation of Public Sector Banks is aimed at having strong banks rather than having large number of banks in the industry. Banking Industry has seen a number of changes over the last 5 decades. Five Associate Banks of State Bank of India viz. State Bank of Bikaner and Jaipur; State Bank of Mysore; State Bank of Travancore; State Bank of Hyderabad and State Bank of Patiala merged with their parent bank i.e. SBI on $1^{st}$ April 2017. On the same day, state owned Bharatiya Mahila Bank also merged with SBI. With the merger of associate banks, India's largest Public Sector Bank SBI became one of the top 50 Banks in the world. In 2019 government of India announced that eight national bank merger in other twelve national banks.

**Advantages of M and A in Indian Banking Sector:**

Merger is generally accepted to promote synergies. The basic idea is that the combined entity will create more value than the individual banks operating independently.

(i) Economies of Scale and Scope
(ii) Greater efficiency
(iii) Leveraging technology
(iv) Managerial efficiency
(v) Changing / Liberal Laws
(vi) Diversification
(vii) Improved market reach and Industry visibility
(viii) Increase Revenue
(ix) Sick banks survived after merger
(x) Enhanced branch network geographically
(xi) Larger customer base (rural reach)
(xii) Increased market share
(xiii) Attainment of infrastructure

**Issues in M and A:**

(i) Bank employees feel personally threatened by mergers and acquisitions, which are not considered to be justified and necessary entrepreneurial activities conducive to enhanced quality banking services.

(ii) The uncertainty that creates stress for employees rather than the actual changes associated with the merger.

(iii) Communication and a transparent change process are important. Leaders need to be competent and trained in the process of transforming organizations to ensure that individuals within the organization accept the changes prompted by a merger.

(iv) Poor merger results are often attributed to HRM and organizational problems and that several factors related to maintaining workforce stability are identified as important in managing HRM risk.

(v) Change management strategies on acceptance of cultural change by individuals occur due to merger.

(vi) A carefully planned, employee-centered communication programme, together with a good level of employee relations, seem to form the basis for a successful outcome as far as employee relations in the face of mergers and acquisitions is concerned.

**Table 2.6: List of some Banks which Merged Since Liberalization**

| Sr. No. | Target Bank | Acquirer Bank | Year |
|---|---|---|---|
| 1 | Bank of Thanjavur Ltd. | Indian Bank | 1990 |
| 2 | Parur Central Bank Ltd. | Bank of India | 1990 |
| 3 | Purbanchal Bank Ltd. | Central Bank of India | 1990 |
| 4 | New Bank of India | Punjab National Bank | 1993 |
| 5 | Bank of Karad Ltd. | Bank of India | 1993 |
| 6 | KashiNath Seth Bank | State Bank of India | 1996 |
| 7 | Punjab Co-op Bank Ltd. | Oriental Bank of Commerce | 1997 |
| 8 | Bari Doab Bank Ltd | Oriental Bank of Commerce | 1997 |
| 9 | Sikkam Bank Ltd. | Union Bank of India | 1999 |
| 10 | Times Bank India | HDFC Bank Ltd. | 2000 |
| 11 | ICICI Bank | ICICI | 2001 |
| 12 | Benaras State Bank Ltd. | Bank Of Baroda | 2002 |
| 13 | Nedungadi Bank Ltd. | Punjab National Bank | 2003 |
| 14 | Bank of Madura | ICICI Bank | 2004 |
| 15 | Global Trust Bank Ltd. | Oriental Bank of Commerce | 2004 |
| 16 | Bank of Punjab | Centurion Bank | 2005 |
| 17 | IDBI Bank | IDBI | 2005 |
| 18 | United Western Bank | IDBI | 2006 |
| 19 | Sangli Bank | ICICI Bank | 2007 |
| 20 | Centurian Bank of Punjab | HDFC Bank | 2008 |

**Source:** Indian Journal of Commerce and Management Studies, Volume III Issue 1, Jan. 2012.

## POINTS TO REMEMBER

- The primary functions of bank includes :
  - (a) Receiving deposits.
  - (b) Accommodation of loans and advances.
- The secondary functions of bank includes :
  - (a) Agency functions. (b) Public utility functions.
- Modern trends in Private Sector Banks :
  - (a) Focus on retail banking. (b) Increasing banking footprint.
  - (c) Financial inclusion.
  - (d) E-payments and mobile banking.
  - (e) ATM outsourcing.

- Types of Bank Accounts :
  - (a) Saving Account. (b) Current Account
  - (c) Fixed Deposit Account.
- Recent Trends in Indian Banking Environment :
  - (a) Emergence of E-banking (b) E-wallents
  - (c) Bank mergers and amalgamations

## QUESTIONS FOR DISCUSSION

1. Describe the various primary functions of bank.
2. Describe the various agency functions of bank.
3. Describe the public utility functions of bank.
4. Explain the structure of Indian Banking System.
5. Explain the reforms of Banking Sector in India.
6. Explain the various types of bank accounts.
7. Explain procedure and operation of savings bank accounts.
8. Describe the recent trends in Indian Banking Environment.
9. Write short notes on :
   - (a) E-banking. (b) E-wallet.
   - (c) Phases of Banking in India. (d) Payment Bank in India.
   - (e) KYC Norms.
   - (f) Bank Mergers and Amalgamations.

***

Unit **3**...

# Overview of Indian Economy

***Contents ...***



## 3.1 CHALLENGES OF INDIAN ECONOMY

### 3.1.1 Poverty

Poverty is social phenomenon in which the society is unable to fulfil even its basic necessities. When a substantial segment of a society is deprived of the minimum level of living and continues at a bore subsistence level, that society is called to be pleasured with mass poverty. Undeveloped and developing countries exhibit invariably the existence of mass poverty, although poverty also exists even in the developed countries in Europe and America. In modern era the concept of poverty is associated with deprivation of a minimum requirement of living or consumption that is minimum requirements for food, clothing, housing, education, health, etc.

With this regards, generally poverty is divided into two types.

1. Absolute Poverty, 2. Relative Poverty.

**(1) Absolute Poverty:** People are absolutely improver shed of the minimum amounts of foods, clothing, and shelter necessary for survival absorb all of their income and they live aerator's edge existence.

Poverty prefers to a set standard of life which consistent overtime and between countries.

**(2) Relative Poverty:** Resources are so seriously below those commanded by the average individual or family that they are in effect excluded from ordinary living patterns, customs and activities.

**Poverty Line - Need of Redefining:**

Redefining poverty is a deceitful issue. There are two schools of thoughts in India. The first one considers income and calories intake as a basic yardstick for defining poverty while others considers infrastructure as basic yardstick.

**Basic Need Approach:**

Mohan Guruswamy and Ronedd Abrabham have highlighted the distinction between poverty and hunger. Poverty is an economical term and hunger is a physical term. Present poverty line definition depend upon calaries. Moreover, poverty line should be renamed as starvation line. Similarly, definition of poverty line include all the basic needs of human life such as nutrition, health, electricity, cooler fuels, clothing, travelling, social ceremonies etc.

Guruswani and Abraham have made indicators of basic human needs to arrive at a new poverty line for India. Basic needs of human life calculation are based on the basic needs of minimal level. The minimum costs on the consumptions of basic needs approach workout to be ₹ 840/- per month and ₹ 4,200/- per month per family. It is guide as balanced nutritious diet ₹ 573/-, Health Insurance expenditure ₹ 30/-, Clothing ₹ 17/-, Energy consumption ₹ 55/-, Miscellaneous Expenditure ₹ 164.

**S. Mahendra Dev and C. Ravi's Redefined Poverty line:**

S. Mahendre Dev and C. Ravi's accounted population of below poverty line by including expenditure of health and education. These both economist studied and concluded that the rural poverty line increase by private health and education expenditure from ₹ 358 to ₹ 392 while urban poverty line increase from ₹ 539 to ₹ 623, due to these reason poverty line increased from 27.5 percent to 35.8 percent, raise to 8.3 percent due to private expenditure on health and education (minimum level).

**Report of Expert Group:**

Prof. S. D. Tendulkar, former Chief Economic Advisor to Prime Minister, submitted report of expert group in 2009. He was Chairman of these group. According to expert group, the poverty line defined in terms of per capita total consumer expenditure at 1973-1974 market price. Moreover, the Poverty Line Basket (PLB) of goods and services keeping unchanged, which is an basis of 1973-74. PLB derived that, the per capita income as calories norms of 2400 calories for rural area and 2100 calories in urban area. But some of them criticize on Tendulkar report, that which consumption pattern applied from expert group, which is three decade ago, Crud Price Adjustment for prices was not plausible and this group assumed that the government made expenditure on social service i.e. health and education, it means this group ignore health and education.

**Table 3.1: Poverty Line Ratio (in percent)**

| Year | Poverty Head Count Ratio | | |
|---|---|---|---|
| | Rural | Urban | Total |
| 1993-94 | 50.1 | 31.8 | 45.3 |
| 2004-05 | 41.8 | 25.7 | 37.2 |
| 2009-10 (Planning Commission Note) | 33.8 | 20.9 | 29.8 |

**Source:** Various report

In India, poverty has declined substantially in recent decades. According to the NSSO data for the year 2004-05, poverty level in India has come down to 21.8% as compared to 36 per cent in 1993-94. In urban areas, the level fell from 23.6 per cent in 1999-2000 to 21.7 per cent in 2004-05 while in rural areas, the poverty level came down from 27.1 per cent to 21.8 per cent during the same period. Kerala continues to be at the top of various indicators showing a high quality of life. Tamil Nadu, Maharastra and Rajasthan are among those making good progress over the period. The poorest states are Orissa, Bihar, Chatisgarh and Madya Pradesh with poverty ratio of 46.4 per cent, 41.4 per cent, 40.9 per cent and 38.3 per cent respectively. The Global Multidimensional Poverty Index-2018 released by the UN noted that 271 million people moved out of poverty between 2005-06 to 2015-16 in India. The poverty rate in the country has nearly halved, falling from 55% to 28% over the ten-year period. Still a big part of the population in India is living Below the Poverty Line. As per Tendulkar Committee this estimation is around 21.9% of the total population of the country.

However, as per report of expert groupwhich showed in above table, there were 45 percent population below poverty line, of these 50.1 percent and 31.8 percent rural and urban people were below poverty line in 1993-94 respectively. Moreover, in 2004-05, which was quiet reduced to 37.2 percent, of these 41.8 and 25.7 percent rural and urban people were below poverty line respectively. According to press note issued by Planning Commission in March 2012, there were 33.8 percent rural people and 20.9 percent urban people were below poverty line and total below poverty line percentage of India has come down to 29.8 percent in 2009-2010.

**Measurement of Poverty:**

Several economists and also organisations conducted the studies to estimated the incidence of poverty in terms of income distribution and consumption etc. Let us discuss concept of poverty.

- *Osha had defined minimum needs in term of physical survival. He had estimated the number of below poverty line on the basis of minimum calorie intake per capita per day. The average calorie requirements 2250 per capita per day. This entailed monthly estimated to involve per capital per day expenditure of ₹ 15 to 18 in urban areas and ₹ 8 to 11 in rural area. In 1960-61 there were total 190 million people (44%) lived below poverty line. Out of these 184 million (51%) people lived in rural area and 6 million (7%) in urban area. Which has increase to total 289 million (70%) rural people lived below poverty in 1967-68.*

**P. D. Osha's Estimate of Poverty**

- *Bardhan argued that GNP deflator includes both agriculture and manufactured commodities if understate the rise in prices paid by rural people because their budget contains smaller proportion of manufactures than the national average. Burdhan stated that, ₹ 15 at 1960-61 prices to be important consumption expenditure rural area. As per his opinion poverty increased from 36 percent to 54 prcent during 1960-61 to 1968-69.* **- P. K. Bardhan Estimate**
- *B. S. Minhas stated about poverty in rural areas during 1956-57 to 1967-68. It was observed that poverty has been steadily reduced from 65 percent to 50.6 percent from 1961-62 to 1967-68. The data showed that in 1968-69, rural poverty was 55 percent and urban poverty was 41 percent.* **- B. S. Minhas Estimate**

- *In 1963-64, Costa noted that 104 million people of destitution and 162 million people of below poverty line, it was 34.9 percent.*

  – **E. P. W. Da Costa's Estimate**
- *Dandekar and Rath rejected the confirm minimum income of ₹ 240 per capital per annum. They both were suggested ₹ 180 per capita per annum for rural people and ₹ 270 for urban population at 1960-61 prices. Which was increased to ₹ 324 and ₹ 486 per capital per annum for rural and urban population at 1968-69 prices respectively. In 1960-61, rural poverty was 40 percent and urban poverty was 50 percent.* – **Dandekar and Rath Estimate**
- *Ahluwalia emphasis regarded to poverty line at ₹ 15 for rural and ₹ 20 for urban area 1960-61 prices.According to this estimation 54.1 percent population below poverty line in 1956-57 which had declined to 38.9 percent in 1960-61. This study covered the period of 1957-58 to 1973-74. Moreover 1973-74 about 46.1 percent population was below poverty line.* – **M. S. Ahluwalia Estimate**
- *Six Five Year Plan gave priority to poverty alleviation programme. This planning commission accepted per capita intake 2400 catories in rural area and 2100 calories in urban area. The estimated cost are ₹ 70 and ₹ 88 in rural and urban area respectively. This commission indicate that, 48.13 percent people were below poverty line in 1977-78 which had declined to 37.4 percent in 1983-84.* - **Sixth Five Year Plan**
- *According to Seventh Plan report, the poverty line at 1984-85 prices per capital income monthly expenditure has been estimated to be ₹ 107 in rural areas and ₹ 122 in urban areas. The percentage of people below the poverty line is expected to decline to 26 percent at the end of seventh plan.* – **Seventh Five Year Plan**
- *The United Nation Development programme has made study regarding to poverty of India in 1992. As per UNDPs estimation India was around 350 million people below poverty line which is about 40 percent of India's population.* - **UNDP, Estimation (1992)**

**Causes of Poverty:**

**(1) Low Productivity of Agriculture:** India is a largely agriculture country. But still Indian agriculture face the problem of land frequented and subdivided, unavailability of proper banking network. Moreover, after new economic reforms government largely negligence towards agriculture sector and all these factors leads to low productivity on the contrary there is successive increase in population. On one side there is low agriculture productivity and other side there is high population which result into poverty.

**(2) Growing Population:** In India there is successive growth of population since 1951. In fact, population increased at a rate of 2.5 percent annually. Therefore, economic situation has adversely affected in two ways, first increasing the number of labour force and secondly reducing the available resources. Moreover averagely more than 17 million people are added every year which rises demand for consumption of goods considerably but on the side income level of people is low with this fact some people can not getting sufficient goods and basic necessities, this situation often called as poverty.

**(3) Unemployment:** Unemployment is another cause of poverty. The continuous expedition working force of unemployed due to higher population. Therefore the job seeker are increasing as high growth rate and they are search employment opportunities, in industrial area. On the other side the agriculture disguised unemployment increased in rural area. Consequently, in both, rural as well urban areas populations income are low, and the result is increase poverty.

**(4) Resources are Under Utilised:** Underutilisation of natural resources have resulted in low production in agriculture sector. This brought down their standard of living, consequently creating poverty in country.

**(5) Higher Level of Prices:** In recent years inflation rate is higher and it is continuously increasing, due to these reason consumer and capital goods prices are increasing, which affect on lower level income people because they cannot offer to fulfil their necessary needs, as the result lower level people consist in poverty.

**(6) Higher Level Disparity:** Generally two class of people are there in society.One is poor people class and second is rich people class. After independence rich people has been getting benefits for all economic activities and other hand lower on people are deprived from economic activities, they find discrimination. As per one report of RBI that 5 percent people get rights on 17 percent wealth of country which is belong to higher class and 20 percent people to get rights on income of country only 9 percent income. It means great economic disparity available in India.

**(7) Social Factor:** The social set up is still backward and is not conducive to faster development. Law of inheritance, caste structure, tradition and customs and also religious people are putting hindrances in the way of faster development and due to this reasons increased the problem of poverty.

**(8) Migration:** Due to low productivity of agriculture, rural working force turn to industrial labour. With this reason, many people migrate rural to urban area, therefore their is made higher level of urbanisation and importantly their is land problem, caused slum area increased, much migrated people lived in slum area, their is cannot getting basic minimum needs, moreover this indicate urban poverty.

**(9) New Economic Policy:** Government adopted new economic policy in 1991, which accepted three concept i.e. globalisation, liberalisation, privatisation. These concept affect on several sector like agriculture, small scale industry, other primary sector. In reforms period multinational corporations increased in India due to globalisation consequently many small scale industries are closed considerably more working force were through outside which find unemployment these situation offered poverty.

Thus, all of these factors consists in poverty, so it is first duty to enable to below poverty line people by set up programme for uplift below poverty line people.

**Measures of Eradication/Removal of Poverty:**

Pandit Jawaharlal Nehru stated that," In a poor country like India here is only poverty to be redistributed" Therefore most important to reduce poverty. Government should initiate measures for remove poverty, followings are some measures,

**(1) Employment Opportunities:** Employment can reduce poverty. Due to more employment opportunities people may be able to meet their basic needs. Therefore in sixth and seventh plan government has started IRDP and IRY plan and RLEGP scheme to eliminate poverty.

**(2) Control Population:** Overpopulation has added people in poverty. However, Government wants to initiate strong policy to reduce poverty. Government want to do compulsory family planning, spread the family planning techniques increases the level of general education and sex education, improve quality of health, spread education for women etc.

**(3) Social Security Programme:** The various social security schemes like Workmen's Compensation Act, Maternity Benefit Act, Provident Fund Act, Employees State Insurance Act, and other benefits in case of death, disability or diseases while on duty can make a attack on poverty.

**(4) Spread Education:** Education develop skill and knowledge and give sprit. So government introduce literacy mission for increase literacy rate, make effective Act i.e. for education, strongly initiate Serva Shiksha Abhiyan, give scholarship to students, to launch many programmes / schemes etc, with these several facilities of education increase standard of living and it can be help to reduce poverty.

**(5) Industrialization:** Faster industrial growth reduce poverty. Industry increases job opportunities. Moreover small scale and cottage industries can help to create employment in rural areas especially in hilly, mountainous and backward region. At this point of view Government has introduce new industrial policy for rural development.

**(6) Land Reforms:** Zamindari System abolished by legislature. Moreover government made act of land reforms, it is not proper implemented. If these reforms implemented seriously, it would yield better result regarding increasing income and reducing poverty.

**(7) Well set-up of Cooperative Sector:** Co-operative sector is one of the best sector to develop economy of rural area. First Co-operative Act made in 1904, there was British empire. In 21$^{st}$ century Cooperative sector completed hundred years but in this large period Co-operative sector had not progress because of several reason i.e. politics, capital untrained staff, no connection between other co-operative institutions, overdue of loan etc. If all of these problems reduce and once more co-operative sector set up in rural area, it will be a help to increase living of standard of people.

**(8) Uplift of Rural Area:** Majority of the Indian population lives in villages. These population generally belongs to landless agriculture labourers, small marginal farmers, scheduled caste, scheduled tribes etc. These people live in below poverty line. Therefore Government introduce certain schemes for upliftment rural people like Indira Awas Yojana, drinking water scheme, road development corporation, primary health centres, Primary schools etc. It will help to reduce poverty.

**(9) Promote to Unorganised Sector:** Liberalisation has focus on 8 percent of labour force which is engaged in organised sector. But the need is to take care of the 92 percent of labour force which is engaged in unorganised sector. It means liberalization fruits have not adequately reached to the poor people. The government should give priority to remake of unemployment land recognize write to work as a base of human right.

### 3.1.2 Employment

The economic reforms implemented since 1991 have accelerated the Development process and generated more employment opportunities in different sectors. The post reforms period has witnessed substantial changes in the structure of employment. The primary sector comprising Agriculture and the allied activities has declined. There has been a marginal increase in the share of the secondary sector. But the tertiary sector registered a sustained increase in the share of the employment. The other noticeable changes in the employment front are an increase in the share of self employment and fall in the causal employment. The regular employment has not increased as expected.

**Employment Trends in India:**

The size of employment in India depends to a great extension on the level of economic development. Therefore, when a country makes economic progress it expands the employment opportunities. In India, during the planning period, production has expanded in all the sectors of economy. In response to the economic development on the absolute level of employment has also increased. The economic growth has made it completely oblivious to possible conflict between economic growth and employment. Hence, in recent year's economic growth in India has been mostly "jobless" and sometimes even "Job loss."

However, details on employment trends are available from various Rounds of the NSSO. Information on employment trends for the period 1993-94 to 2011-12 is presented in following table.

**Table 3.2: Trends of employment and unemployment in India**

**(in million)**

| | 1993-1994 | 1999-2000 | 2004-05 | 2009-10 | 2011-12 |
|---|---|---|---|---|---|
| Labour force | 381.94 | 406.85 | 468.73 | 472.32 | 483.75 |
| Work force | 374.45 | 397.88 | 457.56 | 462.49 | 472.91 |
| Unemployed | 7.49 | 8.97 | 11.17 | 9.84 | 10.84 |
| Unemployment rate | 2.0 | 2.2 | 2.4 | 2.1 | 2.2 |

**Source:** Book-Wages, Employment and Social Security in India, 2019

Table Indicates that more than 23 million jobs were created during the period of 1993-94 to 1999-2000 and 60 million job were created in the period of 1999-200 to 2004-05 and the labour force increased by 25 million over the period 1993-94 to 1999-2000 and by 62 million over the period 199-2000 to 2004-05 to 2009-10 to 2011-12 recorded an increase of 11.43 million people in the labour force. As against the labour force of 381-94 million in 1993-94 and workforce was 374.45 million which implies that the number of unemployed people was 7.49 million two year period 2009-10 to 2011-12 only around 11 million jobs were created.

**Employment and Unemployment Situation in India**

**(a) Labour Force Participation Rate:**

The labour force participation rate indicates about the percentage of population who are already engaged in any kind of work and those who are ready to work given the employment opportunity. The overall labour force participation rate (LFPRs) based on NSS usual status (includes both principal and subsidiary) shows that there has not been any steady decline or increase during the last three and half decades but it was fluctuating between 40 to 44 percent. However, a close look at the trend shows that during 1970s the LFPR had increased to its highest ever in 1977-78 and began to decline thereafter. During the 1980s decline in WPR continued till late 1990s. Between 1987-88 and 1993-94, although there was marginal increase in LFPR, there was a sharp decline of 2 percentage points between 1993-94 and 1999-2000. But the LFPR increased again between 1990-2000 and 2014-2015 with sharp increase of 2.5 percentage points. Again during 2016-2017 the LFPR has declined by 1.9 percentage points from the level of 2014-2015. In fact the sharp decline in LFPR during 1990s could be partly due to increasing attendance rate in educational institutions. The same explanation may not withstand in the LFPR revival scenario given the continuous increase in the enrolment. Therefore one may have to search elsewhere the explanation for fluctuations in LFPR in the recent past.

**(b) Worker Population Rate (WPR):**

In India there were about 459 million workers during 2014-2015 consisting of 42 per cent of the country' total population and the workforce has increased to 461.4 million in 2016-2017. The measure of work participation rate presents the percentage of persons who actually worked or employed in the total population. Work participation rate (WPR) excludes the percentage of unemployed from the labour force participation rate (LFPR).

The trend in work participation rate during the last three and half decades shows that there has not been any sharp decline or increase; it remained between 40 to 42 per cent. But a close look at the trend shows a similar pattern observed in the case of LFPR. Clearly, during 1970s the WPR had increased to its highest ever and during the 1980s there was a decline that continued till late 1990s. The WPR declined to its lowest ever to 39.7% in 1999-2000 and revived between 1999-2000 and 2014-2015 with an increase of 2.3 percentage points. But, it declined to 45% in 2016-2017.

**(c) Level of Unemployment:**

The unemployment rate in India is measured in three ways based on National Sample Survey (NSS) data: based on usual status (US), current weekly status (CWS) and current daily status (CDS). The unemployment rate based on usual status indicates the magnitude of the persons unemployed for a relatively longer period and approximates to an indicator of the chronically unemployed.

Unemployment of workers categorized as usually employed, caused by seasonal fluctuations in the labour market. The "daily status" concept gives an average picture of unemployment on a day during the survey year. Unlike US and CWS which refer to unemployed persons, CDS refers to the person days unemployed8.

Unemployment is a daunting problem for both the developed and developing countries. India is one of those developing countries which continue to have the problem of unemployment and underemployment despite continuous policy emphasis and programmes.

The locational difference in terms of rural-urban unemployment rates shows an unusual pattern when compared to many other socio-economic indicators. It is observed that the unemployment rate is higher among urban labour force when compared to the rural ones. This pattern has been similar in three alternative concepts of unemployment and it has continued for the last three decades. When it comes to gender (i.e. male/female) differences, the unemployment rate based on weekly and daily status shows that it is higher among the female labour force than their male counterparts but based on usual status there has not been any clear trend over the period for usual status.

The unemployment rate by fiver year interval age groups shows that it is the highest among the younger cohorts especially 15 to 24 years age cohorts. In other words, the incidence or instances of those who are willing to work and available for the labour market but unable to find the work or employment is higher among the young (below 30 years) when compared to their seniors (30 + age). It is highest among the 20 to 25 years age cohorts

**Causes of Unemployment:**

Unemployment, of urban as well as rural area is a complex problem due to various factors. The major causes are the following.

**(1) Population Growth:** Growing population is a important cause of unemployment. Indian population has increase near by 2 crore per year. Because of growing population increase in number of labour force and reduce available resources. Moreover, increasing trend of population, demanded employment opportunity but economy can not provide employment opportunity to all people.

**(2) Poverty:** According to NSS 66th Round, 29 percent people live below poverty line. They are poor because they are unemployed. Moreover, developing countries consist of vicious circle of poverty, which in turn influences the pattern of employment opportunities in the country. Being poor a person does not make any gainful use of existing resources.

**(3) Inadequate Employment Growth:** India has neglected employment planning. The public sector annual employment growth rate of organised sector declined to −0.60 percent during 1994 to 2004, it remained negative during 2004 to 2009 at −0.56 percent while in private sector employment rate was 0.36 percent during 1993-2004, its quite increased to 3.58 percent in 2004 to 2009. However total organised sector employment growth rate increase to only 0.82 percent during 2004 to 2009.

**(4) Slow Growth of Tertiary Sector:** Its called service sector also. The expansion of tertiary sector comprising commerce, trade, transportation, communication, banking, insurance etc. Its provide limited employment opportunities. In developed countries more than 70% people engaged in tertiary sector. Therefore it should develop with fast growth rate for increase employment opportunities in India.

**(5) Technological Change in Agriculture:** In recent year many people used agriculture technology like as tractor, harvest machine etc. Due to this reason create disguised unemployment in agriculture sector. So majority of people turn from agriculture to industry sector, but they are not getting work as per capability. They are remain unemployed. So in India available labour in surplus quantity. Many countries adopted labour intensive technology not only in industry sector but also agriculture sector. Therefore India should accept labour intensive technology for reduce unemployment.

**(6) Regional Disparity:** Regional disparity is another cause of unemployment. Some regions are backward, face the shortage of infrastructure while on the other which regions are advanced, possessed, sufficient resources. This imbalance responsible for increasing unemployment rate in backward region.

**(7) Lack of Vocational Guidance and training facilities:** The lack of vocational guidance and training facilities increase rate of unemployment. There is need of the technical training institutions and other job oriented courses at village level. Majority of people have not technical knowledge and skill. Because of these reason more people of village unemployed in rural India.

**(8) Illiteracy:** According to 2011 census, 74 percent people have illiterate but 26 percent people are not literate. Hence many people have not getting jobs because they are not eligible for any employment apart from agriculture. Thus, illiteracy is the main cause of unemployment.

**Measures for Increase Employment:**

Employment is the pushing factor for economy. So it should have remove unemployment in economy. So followings are some measure which are helpful for decline unemployment.

1. **Rapid Industrialisation:** To solve the problem of unemployment, to remove obstacles of industrialisation and remedy likes in stepping up industrial efficiency. It means that the expansion of existing and the development of new industries is urgently required.

2. **Population Control:** Population in India is rising at a very high speed. Without declining trend of population unemployment can not be reduce. Population increases disguised unemployment in agriculture. Therefore family planning programme should be implemented specially in backward region of the country and it want to make compulsory family planning. Government also made more and more budgetary provision to control population since 1951.

3. **Required Employment Exchange:** The Indian economist, suggest to establish more employment exchange in urban as well as rural area which gives proper guidance and motivate people regarding unemployment.

4. **Extension of Social Sector:** Social sector improves quality of human life, it develop skills, knowledge, thinking power of people. It improve social as well as economic power. Social sector gives priority to education, health, housing, drinking water, sanitation and other social services. It make perfect to getting income and improve living of standard. Therefore government should increase more budgetary provision on social sector because India is still behind western countries. If social sector develops, automatically it help to reduce unemployment rate.

5. **Encouragement to Small Enterprises:** Self employment, small scale industries should be given more priority by providing credit facility, technical training, raw material, infrastructure, market facilities, machineries because it is considerably help to motivate self employment and reduce unemployment.

**6. Labour Intensive Technique:** Prof. Mahanobis adopted capital intensive technique for industrial development during second five year plan. Despite the fact government wants to adopted labour intensive technique, definitely this technique useful to reduce unemployment.

**7. Rural Development Scheme:** Agriculture is the basic occupation of rural area. But in recent years, agriculture sector can not provide employment opportunities. So its urgent needy to introduce rural development and employment opportunities scheme.

**8. Emphasis on Vocational and Technical Training:** The curriculum pursued in campuses should be altered to focus more on practical facets of learning. More institutions need to be recognized that offer vocational courses that will interpret straight into pertinent jobs.

**9. Hopeful Self-employment:** Self-employment should be fortified more with outline of liability free loans and government assistance for funding.

**10. Appropriate Macro Policies:** Appropriate macro policies are important for generating employment. In other words, one has to examine whether macro policies in India are pro-employment and pro-poor in the post- reform period. Trade liberalization is expected to improve exports which can generate employment. However, it depends on whether the benefits percolate to unskilled workers or skilled workers. Moreover, Countries inflation rates, can be more flexible in their policy stance with regard to the adoption of more growth oriented as opposed to stabilization policies. Developing countries should learn from China on agricultural growth, rural non-farm employment, public investment and human development (Rao, 2015). The impact of growth on poverty reduction is quite significant in China.

**11. Improvement in Education:** There are emerging signs that rapid growth can result in shortage of high quality skills needed in knowledge intensive industries. One area of concern is that India is losing edge on the tracking of pure sciences. To continue competitive advantage and ensure a continuous supply of quality manpower, we need large investments in public sector institutions of higher learning. This should be accompanied by fundamental reform of the curriculum as well as service conditions to attract a dedicated and qualified faculty. It means India should improve education system from primary to higher level.

**12. Active Labour Market Policies:** Skill improvement is one of the important things needed in active labour market policies. Expanding capacity through private sector initiatives in higher learning needs to be explored while maintaining quality. Conditions of work and promotion of livelihoods are important for raising the incomes of youth workers. Since majority are in the informal sector, protective measures are also required. Minimum level of social security like life insurance, health insurance have to be given to unorganized workers.

### 3.1.3 Inequality in India

Inequality – whether economic, social or political has been an issue of much debate and discussions both in national and international contexts. The most visible aspect is that of economic inequality -one that entails inequality of opportunity accentuated by gender, ethnicity, disability, and age, among others. Further, economic inequality tends to be associated with lower health achievements, high incidence of crimes and elitist biases of public policy and democratic politics. Economic inequality also has a universal nature – as it is a concern both among the rich and poor countries. According to the 2014 Pew Global Attitudes Survey, in the seven Sub-Saharan African nations polled, over 90% of respondents regard the gap between rich and poor as a big problem; in the United States, almost 80% do. India is now among the countries with the highest level of inequality.

In the context of the acceleration of growth rate of Indian economy, the rise in inequality raises issues of the distribution of gains from the growth.

1. 92% of workers are still engaged in informal employment. Close to 276 million workers live below poverty line of $2 per day, and their bargaining positions have declined despite economy growth.
2. Further, both rural-urban disparities as well as inequality within urban areas in per capita expenditure is growing.
3. Recent data also indicate a growing concentration of per capita incomes at the top during the post-reform period. As the distribution of incomes and expenditures has become more unequal, poor people have not gained sufficiently from rapid economic growth.

**Definition of Inequality:**

**The Cambridge Dictionary**, *"The unfair situation in society when some people have more opportunities, etc. than other people".*

**The UN,** "The state of not being equal, especially in status, rights and opportunities".

**Causes or Drivers of Inequality:**

1. **Wealth Inequality:**

India has huge wealth inequality compared to consumption or income inequality, wealth like land, buildings, agricultural machinery, vehicles and financial assets like shares, debentures and amount outstanding. The 1991 and 2002 All India Debt and Investment Survey (AIDIS) highlighted the large discrepancy in wealth holdings across caste groups as well as occupational groups. The level of wealth per capita was found to be similar to the hierarchy of the caste structure and occupational groups. The inequality based on assets has not only increased since 1991, but it has also been accompanied by increasing divergence in wealth held by disadvantaged groups such as Dalits, tribals and Muslims. Analysis by Credit issue as part of their Global Wealth Report (2017) also confirms the finding of a rapid rise in wealth inequality in the last two decades.

2. **Income Inequality:**

Income is not just the money received through pay, but all the money received from employment (wages, salaries, bonuses etc.), investments, such as interest on savings accounts and dividends from shares of stock, savings, state benefits, pensions (state, personal, company). However, there are inequality in income. India Human Development Surveys (IHDS) indicate that income inequality is not reduced from 2004–05 to 2011–12, however, its marginal increase during this period. The NSSO conducts specialized surveys that provide estimates of income for some categories of workers, which collect information on weekly earnings of waged workers. The data do not include information on the earnings of the self-employed who comprise nearly half of all workers. Thus, wage inequality measures are only a partial reflection of the level of inequality in incomes.

3. **Perspectives from the Field:**

Global reports reveal that growing economic inequalities are largely due to over reliance on capital and finance as the drivers, and neglect of labour. This has happened mainly on account of trade and financial globalization processes that have weakened the bargaining position of relatively immobile labour vis-à-vis fully mobile capital. This has resulted in capital-led growth with widespread unemployment and has contributed to lower costs of labour and exploitation of the workforce in the developing countries. There is a need to support the lower end of the economy (for e.g., enterprises in rural areas) where there is more labour and poverty.

**4. Pursuing Employment Led Growth:**

According to some research this disconnect between growing profits and productive investment is largely because most of the increase in profits tends to go financial sectors, rather than real productive sectors. Also, companies tend to use profits to pay out higher dividends to their investors or invest in financial assets. Furthermore, economic uncertainties tend to restrict investments in real economic activities. This lack of productive investment has adverse consequences especially for developing countries as it impacts not just employment generation and livelihoods, but also the ability to provide the poor with basic needs. Therefore, there is a strong case for policies that seek to ensure more equitable distribution of the gains from economic growth and that promote wage and employment-led growth. Employment-led growth as low productivity employment continues to dominate the labour market in both agriculture and other sectors.

Further, providing education and skills to the growing young population and meeting their job aspirations remain challenge. As the pace of migration and urbanization is likely to accelerate in the future, planning urban growth and formulating effective labour market policies will assume greater importance.

**5. Gender and Inequality:**

Increasing economic inequality adversely impacts women. Evidence suggests that there is a strong link between gender equity and economic equality, and that women are more likely to prosper in more egalitarian economies. In a situation where preferences of the rich tend to drive policy outcomes, economic elites are disproportionately likely to oppose egalitarian, pro-worker economic reform. At the same time, there is a strong case for pursuing gender equality to address economic equality. Increasing female employment and earnings tend to reduce household income inequality. Increasing women's employment, flexible workplace policies could offer the additional advantage of boosting economic growth. At present, India faces declining participation of women in work due to the lack of appropriate employment opportunities. In the wake of rising educational levels, the coming years will witness a surge in the number of educated women, many of them will be graduates or more. At present, qualified women enjoy much higher labour force participation rate than average. The country has unfortunately not been able to create enough jobs even for the limited number of educated females in the workforce. This is reflected in the very high rates of unemployment of young women—around 23 per cent among 15 to 29 year-old women, which is double that of their male counterparts. So the challenge for creating suitable employment opportunities for the youth bulge is particularly acute with regard to young women.

### 6. Technology and Innovations:

Technology has caused inequality by favoring the high skill workers. However, advancing technologies has the potential to further human development and reduce inequality. For instance, in order to increase competiveness in the global markets, the cost of production can be substantially brought down by investing in technological innovation and not by the usual method of by saving on labour costs and impoverishing workers. Technology has an important leveraging role to play in facilitating human development through ushering in information rich and diversified economy. The health, globalization and the threat of digital exclusion and environmental sustainability can be addressed by investing in Science and Technology backed by the appropriate policies.

### 7. Growth of Economic Factors and Inequality:

India is the world's second largest emerging economy, with 15% of the global labour force, and an impressive growth record over the last two decades. However, rapid growth has not transformed the labour market and employment conditions in the country. Employment grew merely by 0.5% per annum from 2004-05 to 2011-12 - the period that saw the highest growth of GDP by 8.5% per annum. Further, both rural–urban disparities as well as inequality within urban areas in per capita expenditure are growing. A growing concentration of per capita incomes at the top during the post-reform period. As the distribution of incomes and expenditures has become more unequal, poor people have not gained sufficiently from rapid economic growth.

### 8. Human Development and Inequality:

Education, health, housing, drinking water, family and child care, nutrition etc., affects the state's capacity to intervene in improving the physical infrastructure required to make it available to a larger population group. These are further exacerbated by the relative position of the households in the social hierarchy with disadvantaged social and religious groups further lagging behind in outcomes on human development. Despite impressive economic growth in recent times, India continues to lag behind in terms of improvement in hunger and nutrition indicators. India's very unequally distributed human capital are undoubtedly putting upward pressure on inequality. Poor human development attainments linked to poverty contribute to an inequitable growth process and lost economic opportunities for India's poor. Human development services are much better in urban areas, and there are differences in the people development across different regions.

### 9. Regional Inequality:

Economic policy and reform began in India in the 1980s, and continues today. Prior to the extensive introduction in 1991 of the new economic policy, as it came to be known, there was widespread apprehension that liberalization and excessive reliance on market forces would lead to increase in regional, rural-urban and vertical inequalities in India. The issue is still under debate. There was a sharp increase in regional inequality in India during the 1990s. In 2002-2003, the per capita Net State Domestic Product (NSDP) of the richest state, Punjab, was about 4.7 times of Bihar. This has been highlighted by Ghosh and Chandrasekhar (2003), who showed that inter-state inequality increased sharply in India during the reform period. The basic hierarchy of the Indian states remained the same during the reform period, with Punjab, Haryana and Maharashtra at the top, and Bihar and Orissa at the bottom. They also noted that the gap between the richest and poorest states opened up considerably after 1990-1991.

### 10. Fiscal Policy Measures:

The fiscal policy measures initiated in the reform period did not allow the government to build up productive capacity in the economy. Lack of public investment dampened aggregate demand, negatively affected private investments, created infrastructure bottlenecks to future growth, and adversely affected the provision of important public services. Moreover, in a developing country, where capital expenditure on infrastructure and social services tends to crowd in private investment, reduced expenditure on these sectors led to the crowding out of private investment. As a result of reduced public and private investment, there was inadequate productive employment generation, both in rural and urban areas. This was a key factor behind the increased inequality and slow down of poverty reduction in the country.

**11. Liberalization of Foreign and Domestic Investment:**

Extremely skewed inter-state distribution of domestic and foreign direct investment (FDI) has also contributed to increased inter-regional disparities in India. State-wise data can be seen that the top 10 Indian states attracted more than 63 per cent of total foreign direct investment in India. In contrast, the bottom 10 states together received less than 1 per cent of total FDI. There is also a strong regional disparity in the pattern of FDI flows, with the southern and western states faring much better than the other parts of the country. Three southern states (Andhra Pradesh, Karnataka and Tamil Nadu) received more than 20 per cent of total FDI, while Maharashtra and Gujarat (both in Western India) received 17.35 per cent and 7.7 per cent of FDI respectively. In contrast, the seven North-Eastern states together received only 0.03 per cent of total FDI during the same period. This unequal distribution of FDI across states in India is not unexpected, as FDI inflows tend toward states with better infrastructure and development. The concentration of FDI in a few pockets in India therefore did not help to reduce inequality during the reform period.

**12. Trade Liberalization:**

Trade liberalization is essentially inequitable in nature since it distributes income in favour of the export sector and against the import competing sector. Unless the gains from trade are redistributed, trade liberalization will always change income distribution, which may imply higher inequality. In India, a similar phenomenon can be observed.

**Measures to Reduce Inequality:**

1. India wants fiscal policy, aggregate expenditure and the pattern of public expenditure for reduce inequality.

2. In addition, fiscal federalism relations between the central and provincial governments are very significant in large countries.
3. Methods of raising resources for government expenditure, such as the pattern of taxation.
4. The relationships between growth patterns and the extent and type of employment generated have been extremely important as well.
5. Trade liberalization has dis-equalizing effects; while it provided more opportunities for some export activities. There were adverse effects for those employed in import-competing sectors, especially in small-scale activities.
6. FDI patterns have tended to reinforce existing inequalities, possibly even more than domestic investment.
7. Social security scheme guaranteeing to each individual a minimum standard of economic welfare.
8. The Government may provide equal opportunities to all rich and poor in getting employment or getting a start in trade and industry.
9. The reducing inequalitities between the big and small farmers, ceiling on agriculture land holdings can be imposed.

### 3.1.4 Informal Sector in India

The term 'informal sector' came in a broader sense in the academic literature only after the visit of International Labour Organization (ILO) Employment Mission to Kenya in 1972. The statistics show that informal employment plays a significant role in the global labour market. Two billion workers, representing 61.2 per cent of the world's employed population, are in informal employment. Half of the world's employed population work informally in non-agricultural activities. The level of socio-economic development is positively related to formality. Emerging and developing countries have substantially higher rates of informality than developed countries. The informal sector comprises the largest component of informal employment in all regions. When the share of informal employment is disaggregated by sex, men (63.0 per cent) have higher rates of informal employment than women (58.1 per cent) around the world, but there are actually more countries (55.5 per cent) where the share of women in informal employment exceeds the share of men. Women are more exposed to informal employment in sub-Saharan Africa, the Latin American countries and most low- and lower-middle income countries. They are more often found in the most vulnerable situations. Young people and older persons are found to be more affected by informality than persons aged between 25 and 64. The level of education is another key factor affecting the level of informality. Globally, increases in the level of education are related to decreases in the level of informality. People living in rural areas are almost twice as likely to be in informal employment (80.0 per cent) as those living in urban areas (43.7 per cent). The agricultural sector by nature is the sector with the highest level of informality (93.6 per cent) around the world. The industry (57.2 per cent) and service (47.2 per cent) sectors have relatively less informality.

The Indian Economy is characterized by the existence of a vast majority of informal or unorganized labour employment. More than 90 per cent of workforce and about 50 per cent of the national product are accounted by the informal economy. A high proportion of socially and economically underprivileged sections of society are concentrated in the informal economic activities. According to survey of NSSO in 2004-05, in rural areas the share of informal sector workers in each population segment recorded more than 90 percent and the share of female workers (94.50 percent) is more than male workers (90.34 percent).

**Meaning and Definition:**

**The First Indian National Commission on Labour (1966-69)** defined, "Unorganized sector workforce as –those workers who have not been able to organize themselves in pursuit of their common interest due to certain constraints like casual nature of employment, ignorance and illiteracy, small and scattered size of establishments".

**UN Economic and Social Council (ECOSOC),** "Informal workers are defined to include persons whose employment relationship is not subject to labour legislation, social protection and certain employment benefit".

**The National Council of Applied Economic Research-Self Employed Women's Association (NCAER-SEWA)**, "Informal sector based on employment and stated that this sector included all workers in informal enterprises, some workers in formal enterprises, self – employed workers and those doing contract work for informal or formal sector enterprises and contractors".

**National Commission for Enterprises in the Unorganized Sector (NCEUS 2007),** "Unorganized workers consists of those working in the unorganized enterprises or households, excluding regular workers with social security benefits, and the workers in the formal sector without any employment and social security benefits provided by the employers".

**Major Characteristics of Unorganized Workers:**

The unorganized sector is in no way an independent and exclusive sector. It is linked to or in many cases, dependent on the organized sector and the rest of the economy through a variety of linkages such as for raw materials and other output requirements, generation of employment, marketing facilities and so on. Some specific characteristic of unorganized workers are the following.

1. The unorganized labour is overwhelming in terms of its number and range and therefore, they are omnipresent throughout India.
2. As the unorganized sector suffers from cycles of excessive seasonality of employment, majority of the workers does not have stable and durable avenues of employment.
3. As the work place is scattered and fragmented, the workers do the same kind of jobs in different habitations and may not work and live together in compact geographical areas.
4. There is no formal employer-employee relationship existing in the unorganized sector.
5. In rural areas, the unorganized labour force is highly stratified on caste and community considerations while in urban areas, such considerations are much less because bulk of them are basically migrant workers.
6. They are usually subject to a lot of fads, taboos and outmoded social customs like child marriage, excessive spending on ceremonial festivities, etc. which lead to indebtedness and bondage.
7. The workers are subject to severe exploitation by the rest of the society. They work under poor working conditions, get wage much below than in the formal sector and even for closely

comparable jobs where labour productivity is not different. The work status is of inferior quality in terms of both remuneration and employment.

8. Primitive production technologies and feudal production relations are rampant in the unorganized sector and they do not permit or encourage the workers to imbibe and assimilate higher technologies and better production relations. Large scale ignorance and illiteracy are also responsible for such poor absorption.
9. The unorganized workers do not receive sufficient attention or protection from the trade unions.

**The Characteristics of the Informal Sector Enterprises:**

**(a) Entry:** The informal sector enterprises can be started very easily, in some cases, without license or without registration. They need not follow the legal formalities like formal sector entrepreneurs. There is no need for obtaining certificate of commencement of business or certificate of incorporation in the case of many informal sector units to start the activity. Moreover, it can be started with fixed location or variable location. The business units can be closed at the time of crisis without informing the same to any of the officials or institutions. However, sociological research on street trading, shoe-shining, sale of lottery tickets, small-scale retailing and manufacturing had shown that entry to these activities might be quite restricted, particularly where location advantage would be a major determinant of earnings. Sometimes, skill requirements constitute a barrier to entry as with say, radio repairing, but this is more a technological than an institutional barrier. The institutional factors are more important for the informal sector.

**(b) Scale of Operations:** All the units in informal sector are small in size and more in number. The degree of smallness can be identified by observing the employment in the enterprise. From the empirical point of view, registration would be considered as a good base for demarcating the informal sector. Therefore, the cut-off point of employment could be less than ten in the case of an enterprise operating without power. In general, single worker establishments or self-employed workers would be found more in this sector. Though the small units have some advantages they have their limitations.

**(c) Ownership:** The formal sector is characterized by high degree of ownership and control of industry by certain group of people. As a result, the employees might be absorbed from different parts of the country and world. An informal sector unit has entirely indigenous ownership of its means of production. The proprietor would organize and control the activities of the enterprise. The informal sector operators would not have the same access to credit facilities as their formal counterparts. This obviously would limit the scale of operations. Sometimes, a limited number of casual employees might be employed in an informal sector enterprise with a minimum or less than the minimum wage rate.

**(d) Legal Status:** Many informal activities would involve some degree of illegality. Hawking and peddling without any license or prostitution, pick pocketing and thefts are some of the illegal activities involved in the 'irregular' informal sector. The administrative illegality would derive from legal institutions embodying the values of the dominant class and designed to serve their interests. These might be shared by informal sector members who would regard those activities as legitimate. The informal sector would be determined or influenced by the formal sector activities in any region.

**(e) Production Techniques:** The operations of the informal sector are more labour intensive while in formal sector, use of machinery and technology is common. The formal sector activities too could, however, be labour intensive. The distinction between formal and informal sectors on the basis of use of imported foreign technology or indigenous technology appears to be a rather extreme view point, for, even in formal sector cases of import of know how or foreign collaboration would be fewer. The intent of using technology as a variable in distinguishing informal from formal sector is to highlight that the informal sector units are relatively more labour-intensive, predominantly manual and adopt low techniques of production than formal sector enterprises. In fact, informal sector cannot generally absorb high technology.

**(f) Markets and Pricing:** In informal sector, the features of good distribution, storage and other facilities, in addition to the advantages of branding and packaging are generally rare. Even advertisement and promotion activities are relatively low. This sector relies more on personal selling or word of mouth. The prices of the products are generally set by bargaining between the vendor and the customer involved in the transaction.

**(g) Accessibility to the Government:** A step-mother's attitude of the government would be observed in the case of informal sector. Normally, informal sector does not enjoy patronage from government with regard to the availability of capital market, bank finance, foreign technology, imported raw materials, protection from foreign competitions etc. In general, most of the informal units would be operated on pavements, overcrowded centres and streets and odd places due to scarcity of space in cities and towns.

**(h) Labor Markets:** In informal sector, the labour market is unregulated and highly competitive on the supply side. Anyone can enter freely without any restrictions in the informal sector. Most of the migrants are forced to enter into informal sector activities either as full-time or self-employed or casual or part-time employees because of the limited opportunities and procedural formalities barrier in formal sector.

The employment would be protected for the employees in the sense that the wages and conditions enjoyed by workers in the formal sector would not be available to all the job seekers in the market. The protection may arise from the action of trade unions, government or both acting together. The informal sector would include all unregistered commercial enterprises and all non-commercial enterprises that had no formal structure in terms of organization and operations.

**Classification of Unorganized Workers:**

Unorganized workers can be categorized broadly under the following four heads namely:

1. **By Occupation:** Small and marginal farmers, landless agricultural labourers, fishermen, leather workers, weavers, artisans, those engaged in animal husbandry, beedi rolling, labeling and packing, building and construction, brick kilns and stone quarries, sawmills, oil mills, etc. come in this category.
2. **Nature of Employment:** Agricultural labourers, bonded labourers, migrant workers, contract and casual labourers come under this category.
3. **Specially Distressed Categories:** Toddy tappers, scavengers, carriers of head loads, drivers of animal driven vehicles, loaders and unloaders belong to this category.

4. **Service Categories:** Midwives, domestic workers, fishermen and women, barbers, vegetable and fruit vendors, news paper vendors, etc come under this category.

### Employment Trends of Informal or Unorganized Sector:

Globalisation holds out the promise of enhanced economic growth and employment. India has witnessed increase in rate of growth over the year, along with the employment growth. But the type and quality of employment being created has given rise to some concern among the academicians and policy makers. From table 3.1 and Fig. 1.1 it is evident that total employment in informal sector has increased over the year, with only exception in 2009-10, when employment in informal sector was decreased. On the other hand, total number of informal employment was increased during the said period, with modest decrease in 2009-10 and that of formal employment however, do not show any particular pattern. However, its value remains more or less constant as a percentage of total employment (8.8%).

**Table 3.3: Distribution of formal and informal workers by sector (in million)**

| Sector | 1999-2000 | | | 2004-05 | | | 2009-10 | | | 2011-12 | | |
|---|---|---|---|---|---|---|---|---|---|---|---|---|
| | Informal Worker | Formal Worker | Total Worker | Informal Worker | Formal Worker | Total Worker | Informal Worker | Formal Worker | Total Worker | Informal Worker | Formal Worker | Total Worker |
| Informal | 341.28 (99.6) | 1.36 (0.4) | 342.64 (100) | 393.47 (99.6) | 1.43 (0.4) | 394.90 (100) | 375.84 (99.36) | 2.41 (0.64) | 378.28 (100) | 386.02 (99.57 | 1.68 (0.43) | 387.70 (100) |
| Formal | 20.46 (37.8) | 33.67 (62.2) | 54.12 (100) | 29.14 (46.6) | 33.42 (53.4) | 62.57 (100) | 44.77 (53.97) | 38.19 (46.03) | 82.95 (100) | 37.15 (51.09) | 35.58 (48.91) | 72.73 (100) |
| Total | 361.74 91.2 | 35.02 (8.8) | 396.76 (100) | 422.61 (92.4) | 34.85 (7.6) | 457.46 (100) | 420.6 (91.2) | 40.6 (8.8) | 461.2 (100) | 423.17 (91.91) | 37.26 (8.09) | 460.43 (100) |

**Source:** NCEUS (2007), IOSR Journal of Business and Management (IOSR-JBM), Volume 20, Issue 4, Vol. III April. 2018

The table indicates that between 1999-2000 and 2011-12, the total work force in India expanded from 396.76 million to 460.43 million and majority of them are engaged in the informal sector. The concept of informal worker is based on the personal characteristics of the worker rather than enterprises. A major part of the workers engaged in organized sector are also informal workers. The share of informal employment in the unorganized sector is unchanged at 99.5 percent throughout the decade. Thus a large number of workers in the formal sector are informal in nature. They do not have any social security, job security and other benefits which the regular wage employees enjoy in the formal sector.

**Challenges/Problems Faced by Unorganised Workers:**

1. Unorganized sector are heterogeneous category, as compared to homogenous organized sector.
2. Illiteracy, wage (No guaranteed minimum wages) and poverty.
3. Working women (gender discrimination) – issue of harassment at work place
4. Identification of employer in this sector is difficult.
5. There is no steady, secure and regular employment, work is on contract basis.
6. Bonded labor - they don't complain about harasment if they do their master may remove them.
7. Majority strikes hard for fulfilling basic necessities such as food, clothing and shelter.
8. Lack of unionization of unorganized sector.
9. Absence of regulatory bodies for governing laws and provisions.
10. No social security
11. Vulnerable to diseases

## 3.2 POLICY MEASURES – PROGRAMMES

The Government inter alia, is implementing some programmes to bring about overall improvement in the quality of life of the people through employment generation, strengthening of livelihood opportunities, promoting self employment, skilling of youths, provision of social assistance and other basic amenities. These programmes have direct and indirect bearing on poverty reduction. Besides improving the pace of implementation of these programmes substantially. Followings are the some programmes;

### 3.2.1 Poverty Alleviation Programmes

**(1) National Rural Employment Guarantee Scheme (NREGS):** This National Rural Employment Guarantee Act implement in 2006 in India's 200 most backward districts. This scheme provides 100 days of employment and minimum wages to every rural people. In 2007 it was extended to 130 districts and from 2008 this Act covered all districts.

**(2) Minimum Need Programmes (MNP):** Minimum Need Programme was introduced in the fifth five year plan. This programme provided free and subsidized services and raise productivity efficiency to below poverty line people in rural and urban area. Its basic indicators are primary education, water supply, health, roads connectivity, electricity, housing facilities to provide landless labours. During fifth plan period, it spend ₹ 1038 corers on this scheme. In 1978-80, on ₹ 1147 corers where spend on this scheme.

**(3) National Rural Development Programme (NREP):** NREP provide supplementary employment opportunities to rural people particular during lean period. NREP launched in October, 1980 as Central and State Sponsored (50 : 50) scheme. Main objectives is generating gainful employment and improving overall quality of life in rural area. During sixth plan ₹ 1843 crores spend on this scheme and creating 17,751 lakh mandays work. Of the total employment there were 45 percent people belongs to SC/ST.

**(4) Rural Landless Employment Guarantee Programme (RLEGP):** RLEGP was launched on $15^{th}$ August, 1983 objectives was to expand and improve employment for rural landless, to create productive and durable assets for strengthening rural infrastructure, to improve overall quality of life of rural people. This scheme was fully sponsored by Central Government. During Sixth Plan total 2628 mandays of employment were generated, with expenditure of ₹ 384.74 crores.

**(5) Desert Development Programme (DDP):** This scheme recommended by National Commission on Agriculture in 1977. This programme covered area like :

(a) the hot arid desert i.e. 11 district of Rajasthan, 4 district of Harayana, 3 district of Gujarat and

(b) cold arid desert i.e. Jammu and Kashmir and split subdivision of Lahul and spilt district of HP. The main objectives was controlling further desertification of the desert areas and raising productivity of the local inhabitants. During sixth and seventh plan incurred ₹ 73.55 crore and ₹ 100.17 crore respectively.

**(6) Drought Prone Area Programme (DPAP):** DPAP was launched as an integrated area development programme in 1973. This programme measure for ecological balance and optimum utilization of the land, water, livestock and human resources and to mitigate the effects of drought. DPAP implemented in 615 blocks in 91 districts of 13 states and covering 536 lakh 59 km from 1985-86. It covered total 7.5 crore population. During sixth plan incurred ₹ 377.41 crore. During seventh plan period total 4480 mandays employment created in drought area. In 1990-92, there were ₹ 938.9 crores spend on this scheme total allocation was ₹ 1022.30 crores.

**(7) Training of Rural Youth for Self Employment (TRYSEM):** TRYSEM was launched as a centrally sponsored scheme on August, 15, 1979. The main aim of these scheme is generating employment opportunities for the unemployed educated rural youth and to develop skills and technology in the age group of 18 to 35 rural young for self employment in the broad field of agriculture and allied activities, industry, service sector. Under this programme training and teaching institution were also started with the central assistance. In sixth plan 10-50 lakh youth was proposed whereas 9.4 lakh youths were actually trained. During seventh plan 10 lakh youth was trained of these 47 percent self employed and 12 percent in wage employment. In 1991-92, about three lakh youth were trained. This scheme also promoted to 33 percent women.

**(8) Jawahar Rozgar Yojana (JRY):** JRY introduced in 1989-90, the main purpose is generating more employment in the economy. Now NREP and RLEGP schemes are merged in JRY. This programmes has given higher priority to works which are important poverty alleviation. Under this scheme 492 million mandays have been generated in 1989 against the target of 873 million mandays for the year.

**(9) Integrated Rural Development Programme (IRDP):** IRDP announced in 1976-77, based on the local needs, resources, endowments and potentialities. IRDP has been renamed as District Rural Development Agency (DRDA). In 1978-89 another three schemes integrate in IRDP i.e. Small Farmers Development Agency (SFDA), Drought Prone Areas Programme (DPAP), Command Area Development (CAD). It is centrally sponsored schemes. The major objectives of the IRDP is to raise the production and productivity in agriculture and allied sectors and creating productive assets for improving of the rural people, also improving harvest technology in rural area. At the beginning of this scheme 2000 block covered which has increased to 3500 blocks in 1983. During Sixth plan (1980-83) 3000 families provided specific assistance, of these 20 percent families belongs to SC/ST.

**(10) Prime Minister Integrated Urban Poverty Eradication Programme (PMIUPEP):** PMIUPEP was initiated during 1995-96, with the objective of effective achievement of social goals. This programme carried 5 million urban poor live in 345 class with a population of 50,000 to 1,00,000 each. In 1995-96 ₹ 100 crore has been fixed for this scheme.

**(11) Antodaya Yojana:** This scheme aims at economic upliftment of the poorest of the poor families. The Government of Rajasthan and UP announced this scheme. This scheme adopted 33,000 villages in 1977 and provided facilities to 4,57,000 families in the same year.

**(12) Indira Awas Yojana (IAY):** The genesis of the IAY can be traced to be programme of rural employment which began in 1980s. But IAY was launched during 1985-86 as a sub scheme of RLEGP. Thereafter IAY continued as a sub scheme of JRY. From the year 1993-94 the scope of IAY was expended to cover households below poverty line and SC/ST families in rural areas. The objective of IAY is primarily to help construction/upgrading of dwelling units of members of SC/ST, free bonded labourers. Moreover, other below the poverty line non SC/ST rural households by providing them a lump sum financial assistance. This scheme Central/State (75 : 25) sponsored scheme. This scheme provide ₹ 28,500 grant to rural people in 2008, these grant increased to ₹ 40,000/-. However, after 2012 which is also increased to ₹ 70,000/-. Now Government has providing 168000/- to rural people.

**13. Pradhan Mantri Awaas Yojana-Gramin (PMAY-G):** The rural housing scheme Indira Awaas Yojana (IAY) has been restructured as Pradhan Mantri Awaas Yojana – Gramin (PMAY-G), in line with the government's stated objective of "Housing for All" by 2022. The new scheme PMAY-G are being implemented from the year 2016-17.

**Salient features of PMAY-G:**

(i) Target of construction of 1 crore houses in rural areas from 2016-17 to 2018-19.

(ii) Enhancement of unit assistance from ₹ 70,000 to ₹ 1.20 lakhs in plain areas and from ₹ 75,000 to ₹ 1.30 lakhs in hilly states, difficult areas and IAP districts

(iii) Enhancement of minimum area from 20 to 25 square meter.

(iv) Using SECC-2011 data for identification of beneficiaries.

(v) Facilitation to avail loan of upto ₹ 70,000/- for construction of the house.

(vi) Provision of ₹ 12,000/- as assistance for construction of toilet under Swachh Bharat Mission (G), MGNREGA or any other dedicated financing source over and above unit assistance.

(vii) Support of 90/95 person days in plain areas/hilly states, difficult areas and IAP districts under MGNREGS through convergence.

(viii) House design typologies incorporating disaster resilient features compiled in a compendium PAHAL (Prakriti Hunar Lokvidya).

(ix) Training, assessment and certification of rural masons, as per the Qualification Pack endorsed by National Skill Development Corporation (NSDC) for improvement in construction quality of houses under PMAY-G.

(x) Various innovative initiatives like use of 'AwaasApp' to capture georeferenced, time and date stamped photographs of the house at various stages of construction, and 100% DBT mode of payment have been a breakthrough in implementation of the programme in a transparent manner.

(xi) A total of 34.82 lakh houses have been constructed during 2014-15 to 2015-16 under the erstwhile rural housing scheme Indira Aawas Yojana (IAY). During 2016-17, a total of 32.14 lakh houses have been completed with an expenditure of ₹ 16,074 crore.

**14. Other Programmes:** Many other programmes announced by Government for rural people who are below poverty line. The Prime Minister Yojana (October, 1993), Mahila Samridhi Yojana (October, 1993), National Social Assistance Programme (August, 1995), Swarnajayanti Swarozgar Yojana, New Job Creation Scheme (September, 1993). These Schemes objective is Development of Rural people in India.

Thus, Government has been improving condition of below poverty line people from 1970. But yet it has not achieve at expected level. As per statistics of Government in 2009-10, there were 29.1 percent people were below poverty line in India.

### 3.2.2 Employment Generation Programmes

1. **Mahatma Gandhi National Rural Employment Guarantee Act (MGNREGA):**

It is a flagship programme of the Government, aimed at enhancing livelihood security of the households in rural areas of the country by providing at least one hundred days of guaranteed wage employment in a financial year. MGNREGA has been transformed with highest ever expenditure during FY 2016-17 and several new governance initiatives like Geo-MGNREGA, NeFMS, more independent and empowered system of Social and Internal Audit etc. to ensure growth, accountability and transparency under the programme. Other noticeable developments under MGNREGA are:

(a) **Persondays of employment:** During FY 2016-17, 5.04 crore households have been provided employment in 138.64 lakh works. In the process 235.82 crore person days of employment have been generated.

(b) **Highest completion of work:** On an average, 25 to 35 lakh works get completed every year. However in FY 2016-17, 52.4 lakh works have been completed. The completion rate of works has been quite impressive in FY 2016-17.

(c) **Irrigation potential created:** Around 68% of expenditure has been on agriculture and allied activities which is the highest ever since the inception of the programme.

(d) **Focus on natural Resource Management (NRM)**: About 62% of total expenditure in FY 2016-17 has been on NRM related works as against 49% during FY 2014-15. 30.43 lakh such works have been completed which include 5.79 lakh farm ponds.

(e) **Women participation:** Out of the total employment, 56% employment has been generated for women, which is the highest participation of women since the inception of the programme.

2. **Pradhan Mantri Gram Sadak Yojana (PMGSY):**

The primary objective of PMGSY is to provide connectivity by way of an All-Weather road. Under PMGSY, the unit of programme is a Habitation and not a revenue village or panchayat.

(i) Under PMGSY, the pace of construction of road has reached a record of 130 kms. per day, which is the highest average annual construction rate, in the last 7 years, with a record 47,447 kms of PMGSY roads constructed during 2016-17 thereby connecting

11,641 habitations, which implies providing connectivity of an average of 32 habitations every day, the highest ever in the last 7 years.

(ii) During the last three years (2014-15 to 2016-17), 1, 20,233 km of road length has been completed under PMGSY.

(iii) During 2016-17, "Road Connectivity project in LWE Affected Areas" has been launched for construction of all weather roads in 9 LWE states in 44 worst affected LWE districts and adjoining districts with estimated cost of Rs 11,725 crore. This would be completed by March, 2020.

(iv) **Green Technologies:** PMGSY is aggressively encouraging use of "Green Technologies" and non-conventional materials in rural roads. 4,113.13 kms. of PMGSY roads were constructed using "Green Technologies", in 2016-17 which is substantially higher than 2,634.02 kms achieved during 2014-2016 and 806.93 kms achieved during 2000-2014.

**3. The National Rural Employment Programme (NREP):** NREP was started during sixth plan and was continued in seventh plan, on 1st April, 1989 it was merged in Jawahar Rojgar Yojana (JRY). It was central-State Shared (50 : 50) scheme and it was also wage employment scheme.

**4. The Rural Landless Employment Guarantee Programme (RLEGP):** As on 15th August, 1983, RLEGP initiated with the aim of expanding employment opportunities for the rural landless. It was employment guarantee scheme to landless households for about 100 days work in a year.

**5. Prime Minister Rojgar Yojana (PMRY):** PMRY designed during Eighth five year plan for to provide self employment to more than one million educated unemployment youth. During eighth plan, 7.70 lakh cases sanctioned, the actual disbursement of loans was to ₹ 5.76 lakhs.

**6. The Employment Assurance Scheme (EAS):** The EAS objective was to provide 100 days unskilled manual work at least two members of family in the age group of 18 to 60 years. During 1996-97 to 1999-2000 a total of 1,533.7 million man days employment was generated under this scheme.

**7. Sampoorna Gramin Rojgar Yojana (SGRY):** SGRY started on September 25, 2001, aimed at providing additional wage employment in rural areas. Jawahar Gram Samridhi Yojana (JGSY) and Employment Assurance Scheme (EAS) were integrated with SGRY. In 2005-06, there were 82.18 crore man days of employment were generated under this scheme.

**8. Swarnajayanti Grameen Swarojgar Yojana:** SGSY launched 1st April, 1999, it is only self employment programme for the rural poor. Objective is to being self employed above the poverty line by proved them income generating assets from bank and government subsidy. In 31st December, 2006, their are, 24.38 lakh self-help groups have been formed and total 73.25 lakh persons have been assisted and total outlay was ₹ 16,444 crore.

**9. The Swarana Jayanti Shahari Rojagr Yojana (SJSRY):** SJSRY aims to provide gainful employment to the urban unemployment or underemployed poor through self employment ventures and wage employment. In December 1, 1997 SJSRY launched by Government. It is Central State (75 : 25) 36 sponsored scheme.

### 3.2.3 Agriculture Development Programmes

**1. National Mission for Sustainable Agriculture (NMSA):**

NMSA is envisaged as one of the eight Missions outlined under National Action Plan on Climate Change (NAPCC), NMSA aim at promoting sustainable agriculture through climate change adaptation measures. The major thrust is enhancing agriculture productivity especially in rainfed areas focusing on integrated farming, soil health management, and synergizing resource conservation. Besides, NMSA also a committed target to fulfil National and International commitments on Sustainable Development Goals (SDG) and Intended Nationally Determined Contribution (INDC). All the components of NMSA such as Rainfed Agriculture, Soil Health Management, Organic Farming, etc. have significant role in achieving SDGs and INDC. NMSA as a programmatic intervention caters to Mission Deliverables that focuses mainly on conservation agriculture to make farm sector more productive, sustainable, remunerative and climate resilient by promoting location specific integrated/composite farming systems; soil and moisture conservation measures; comprehensive soil health management and mainstreaming rainfed technologies. NMSA has the following schemes;

**(i) Rainfed Area Development (RAD):** RAD focuses on Integrated Farming System (IFS) for enhancing productivity and minimizing risks associated with climatic variability's. Under this system, crops/cropping system is integrated with activities like horticulture, livestock, fishery, agro-forestry, apiculture etc. to enable farmers not only in maximizing farm returns for sustaining livelihood, but also to mitigate the impacts of drought, flood or other extreme weather events with the income opportunity from allied activities during crop damage. For the Year 2019-20 (B.E), budget provision of ₹ 250.0 crore has been made for implementation of the programme.

**(ii) Pradhan Mantri Krishi Sinchayee Yojana (PMKSY):** The Pradhan Mantri Krishi Sinchayee Yojana (PMKSY) was launched on 1st July, 2015 with the motto of *'Har Khet Ko Paani'* for providing end-to end solutions in irrigation supply chain, viz. water sources, distribution network and farm level applications. PMKSY not only focuses on creating sources for assured irrigation, but also creating protective irrigation by harnessing water rain at micro level through *'Jal Sanchay'* and *'Jal Sinchan'*. Micro irrigation is to be popularized to ensure 'Per drop-More Crop'. PMKSY adopts State level planning and projectised execution that allows States to draw up their own irrigation development based on District Irrigation Plans and State Irrigation Plans.

**PMKSY - Per Drop More Crop (PDMC):**

Department of Agriculture, Cooperation and Farmers Welfare is implementing Per Drop More Crop component of PMKSY, which is operational from 2015-16 in the country. Per Drop More Crop mainly focuses on water use efficiency at farm level through precision/ Micro Irrigation (MI) (Drip and Sprinkler Irrigation). Besides promoting precision irrigation and better on-farm water management practices to optimize the use of available water resources, this component also supports gap filling interventions as Other Interventions like micro level water storage or water conservation/management activities to complement and supplement the source creation. For the Year 2019-20, budget provision of ₹ 3500 crores has been made to implement the Per Drop More Crop component.

**PMKSY (Per Drop More Crop) - Micro Irrigation:**

Since January 2006, the Government of India has been implementing Centrally Sponsored Scheme on Micro Irrigation with the objective to enhance water use efficiency in the agriculture sector. Under the scheme, technological interventions like drip and sprinkler irrigation systems are promoted to encourage the farmers to use them for conservation and saving of water and improved yield. In June 2010, the scheme was up-scaled to National Mission on Micro Irrigation (NMMI), which continued till the year 2013-14. From 1st April 2014, NMMI was subsumed under National Mission on Sustainable Agriculture (NMSA) and implemented as one of the components under "On Farm Water

Management" (OFWM) during 2014-15. From 1st July 2015, the scheme has been subsumed under Pradhan Mantri Krishi Sinchayee Yojana (PMKSY) and implemented as 'Per Drop More Crop (Micro Irrigation)' component of PMKSY.

**Salient Features of the Micro Irrigation Scheme under PMKSY:**

- Under PDMC, Financial Assistance is available up to 55% for small and marginal farmers and 45% for other farmers for adoption of micro irrigation system. The funding pattern between Central Government share and State Govt. share since November 2015 has been 60 : 40 for all states except North Eastern and Himalayan States. For North Eastern and Himalayan States the funding pattern is 90 : 10.
- Under Operational Guidelines of the scheme, indicative/average/ normative cost has been laid down for various crops/lateral spacing and different micro irrigation systems for the purpose of calculating financial assistance. Twenty five (25%) higher cost, over and above the normative cost for all systems has been fixed for North Eastern and Himalayan states for this purpose and 15% for low penetration .
- Scheme is applicable in all states and all districts in the country.
- All horticultural and agricultural crops are covered under the scheme. At least 25% of the funds allocated to the State under scheme are to be used necessarily for agricultural crops.
- At least 50% of the allocation to state is to be utilized for small and marginal farmers, of which, at least 30% has to be women beneficiaries/farmers. Further, 16% and 8% of the total allocation or in proportion of Scheduled Cast (SC)/Scheduled Tribe (ST) population is to be utilized for Special Component Sub-Plan (SCSP) and Tribal Sub-Plan (TSP) respectively.
- Equipments adhering to Indian Standards are only eligible for financial assistance under the scheme.
- Information and Communication Technology (ICT) has been extensively deployed for ensuring transparency in scheme implementation process and for effective monitoring of the programme. PMKSY website has been operationalized at the Central level. In many states also similar websites have been set up by the respective state governments.
- PMKSY has an end to end approach for development of irrigation chain from creation of water resources to field application of water in

an integrated manner. Accordingly, all components of PMKSY are to be implemented in complementation with each other.

**Adoption of Micro Irrigation is Providing Economic Benefits to Farmers:**

Micro irrigation which includes drip and sprinkler irrigation is a proven technology which has gained immense popularity amongst the farmers in India. Strengths of this technology include - efficient deployment of inputs such as water, electricity, fertilizers, labour etc., increase in crop productivity, better quality of produce leading to higher realization of sale price resulting in increased income of farmer and prosperity. With this technology, additional area can be irrigated with the same amount of water compared to conventional method of irrigation. In addition, water deficient, cultivable waste land and undulating land areas can easily be brought under cultivation due to ease of irrigation. With this technology, there is also a good scope for using it in closely spaced crops like rice, wheat, onion, potato etc. Benefits of this technology lead to control of ground and surface water pollution. Micro irrigation technology has a good scope for generation of employment opportunities in rural areas besides arresting migration of farmers to cities.

**An impact evaluation study for Micro Irrigation was carried out in the year 2014 and major findings of the study are:**

- Irrigation cost reduced by 20% to 50% with the average of 32.3%.
- Electricity consumption reduced by about 31%.
- Saving of fertilizers vary from 7% to 42%.
- Average productivity of fruits and vegetables increased by about 42.3% and 52.8%.
- Overall income enhancement of farmers in the range of 20% to 68% with average of 48.5%

The positive outcomes of micro irrigation have made food security effective due to increase in production and productivity of different crops and increased area under irrigation from the same source of water resulting in enhanced nutritional security for the country.

**(iii) Micro Irrigation Fund:** A dedicated Micro Irrigation Fund created with NABARD has been approved with an initial corpus of ₹ 5000 crore (₹ 2000 crore for 2018-19 and ₹ 3000 crore for 2019-20) for encouraging public and private investments in micro irrigation. The main objective of the fund is to facilitate the States in mobilizing the resources for expanding coverage of micro irrigation. MIF would not only facilitate States in incentivizing and mobilizing resources for achieving the target envisaged under PMKSY-PDMC but also in bringing additional coverage through special and innovative initiatives by State Governments. An Advisory Committee has been set up to provide policy direction and ensure effective planning, coordination and monitoring of the Micro Irrigation Fund.

**(iv) Agriculture Contingency Plan:** Central Research Institute for Dryland Agriculture (CRIDA), ICAR has prepared district level Agriculture Contingency Plans in collaboration with state agricultural universities using a standard template to tackle aberrant monsoon situations leading to drought and floods, extreme events (heat waves, cold waves, frost, hailstorms, cyclone) adversely affecting crops, livestock and fisheries (including horticulture). Total 614 district agriculture contingency plans are placed in the 'farmer portal' of the Ministry of Agriculture and Farmers Welfare, Government of India.

**2. Pradhan Mantri Fasal Bima Yojana (PMFBY):**

PMFBY is an actuarial premium based scheme under which farmer has to pay maximum premium of 2% for Kharif, 1.5% for Rabi food and oilseed crops and 5% for annual commercial/horticultural crops and remaining part of the actuarial/bidded premium is shared equally by the Centre and State Government. One of the objectives of the scheme is to facilitate prompt claims settlement. The claims must be settled within two months of harvest subject to timely provision of both yield data and share of premium subsidy by the State Government.

**3. Paramparagat Krishi Vikas Yojana (PKVY):**

It is implemented with a view to promote organic farming in the country.To improve soil health and organic matter content and increase net income of the farmer so as to realise premium prices. Under this scheme, an area of 5 lakh acre is targeted to be covered though 10,000 clusters of 50 acre each, from the year 2015-16 to 2017-18.

**4. National Agriculture Market (e-NAM):**

It provides e-marketing platform at national level and support creation of infrastructure to enable e-marketing. This innovative market process is revolutionizing agriculture markets by ensuring better price discovery. It brings in transparency and competition to enable farmers to get improved remuneration for their produce moving towards 'One Nation One Market'.

**5. National Watershed Development Project for Rainfed Areas (NWDPRA):**

The scheme of National Watershed Development Project for Rainfed Areas (NWDPRA) was launched in 1990-91 based on twin concepts of integrated watershed management and sustainable farming systems.

**Aim:**

(i) Conservation, development and sustainable management of natural resources.

(ii) Enhancement of agricultural production and productivity in a sustainable manner.

(iii) Restoration of ecological balance in the degraded and fragile rainfed eco-systems by greening these areas through appropriate mix of trees, shrubs and grasses.

(iv) Reduction in regional disparity between irrigated and rainfed areas and;

(v) Creation of sustained employment opportunities for the rural community including the landless.

### 3.2.4 Skill Development Programmes

**1. Deen Dayal Antyodaya Yojana National Rural Livelihood Mission (DAYNRLM):**

The DAY-NRLM is aimed at reaching out to all rural poor households estimated at about 9 crore and link them to sustainable livelihood opportunities through organizing them into self-managed institutions, skill and capacity building and enable them to access finance, livelihood services, till they come out of poverty.

(i) Compared to 2.9 lakh SHGs promoted during FY 2013-14, nearly 3.7 lakh and 5.1 lakh SHGs have been promoted during 2015-16 and 2016-17 respectively under DAY-NRLM.

(ii) During 2016-17, 60 lakh households have been brought into SHG network through 5.1 lakh new SHGs taking the total number to 3.86 crore Households and 32.53 lakh SHGs.

(iii) SHGs have accessed ₹ 91381 crore bank credit during 2014-2017 as compared to ₹ 55305 crore bank credit accessed by them during 2011-2014.

(iv) About 950 SHG members have been trained and placed as Banking Correspondents Agents for providing door step banking services to SHG members in rural areas.

(v) Start-up Village Entrepreneurship Programme (SVEP) has been rolled out in 17 States covering 47 blocks with an outlay of ₹ 208 crore for promoting about 84,000 rural enterprises.

**2. Deen Dayal Upadhyaya Grameen Kaushalya Yojana (DDU-GKY):**

DDU-GKY is the Placement Linked Skill Development scheme, implemented in PPP mode. It targets rural youth from poor families in the age group of 15 to 35 years.

(i) Against a target of training 10.50 lakh candidates in FY 2012-2017, a total of 9.38 lakh candidates have been trained and 5.79 lakh candidates placed.

(ii) Out of 1, 62,586 candidates trained during 2016-17, nearly 39 per cent were women.

(iii) Under RSETIS, 60 per cent of candidates trained were women in 2016-17, i.e. out of 444982 candidates trained, 266989 were women.

(iv) 37007 candidates have been trained under Project LIFE (Livelihoods under Full Employment) MGNREGA by Rural Self Employment Training Institutes (RSETIs) and 19327 candidates trained by RSETIs have been linked to credit under PM MUDRA programme.

**3. National Rural Livelihood Mission (Ajeevika):**

It is the skill and placement initiative of Ministry of Rural development. It is a part of National Rural Livelihood Mission (NRLM)–the mission for poverty reduction is called Ajeevika, introduced in 2011. It evolves out the need to diversify the needs of the rural poor and provide them jobs with regular income on monthly basis. Self Help groups are formed at the village level to help the needy.

**4. Pradhan Mantri Kaushal Vikas Yojna:**

The cabinet on March 21, 2015 cleared the scheme to provide skill training to 1.4 million youth with an overall outlay of ₹ 1120 crore. This plan is implemented with the help of Ministry of Skill Development and Entrepreneurship through the National Skill Development Corporation. It will focus on fresh entrant to the labour market, especially labour market and class X and XII dropouts.

## POINTS TO REMEMBER

- **Challenges Faced by Indian Economy :**

  (a) Poverty, (b) Rising Unemployment, (c) Growing Inequality.

- **Major Poverty Alleviation Programmes in India :**

  (a) National Rural Employment Guarantee Scheme (NREGS).

  (b) National Rural Development Programme (NRDP).

  (c) Minimum Needs Programme (MNP).

  (d) Drought Prone Area Programme (DPMP).

  (e) Jawahar Rozyar Yojana (JRY).

  (f) Integrated Rural Development Programme (IRDP).

  (g) Antodya Yojana.

- **Major Employment Generation Programme in India :**

  (a) Mahatma Gandhi National Rural Employment Guarantee ACt (MGNREGA).

  (b) Pradhan Mantri Gram Sadak Yojana (PMGSY).

  (c) Prime Minister Rojgar Yojana (PMRY).

  (d) Sampoorna Gramin Rojgar Yojana (SGRY).

- **Agriculture Development Programmes in India :**

  (a) Rainfed Area Development (RAD).

  (b) Pradhan Mantri Krishi Sinchayee Yojana (PMKSY).

  (c) Per Drop More Crop Scheme.

- **Skill Development Programme in India :**

  (a) Deen Dayal Antyodaya Yojana National Livelihood Mission.

  (b) Deen Dayal Upadhyaya Grameen Kaushalya Yojana.

  (c) National Rural Livelihood Mission.

  (d) Pradhan Mantri Kaushal Vikas Yojana

## QUESTIONS FOR DISCUSSION

1. Discuss the various challenges in Indian Economy.
2. Explain the various causes of unemployment in India.
3. Explain the various causes of inequality in India.
4. Explain characteristics of informal sector enterprises.
5. Describe the various poverty alleviation programme in India.
6. Discuss the various employment generation programmes.
7. Discuss the various agriculture development programmes.
8. Write short notes on :
   (A) Causes of poverty in India.
   (B) Characteristics of unorganised workers.
   (C) Measurement of poverty.

***

# MODEL QUESTION PAPER

**Time : 3 Hours** **Marks : 70**

**Q. 1 Answer the following questions in 300 words (Any one) : (15)**

(a) Explain the role of service sector in Indian economy.

**OR**

(b) Describe the various functions of a bank.

**Q. 2 Answer the following questions in 300 words (Any one) : (15)**

(a) State the challenges to health sector of the Indian economy.

**OR**

(b) Discuss the various challenges of Indian economy.

**Q. 3 Answer the following questions in 200 words (Any two) : (20)**

(a) Explain the challenges of Indian banking sector.

(b) What are the modern trends in private sector banks ?

(c) Describe the various poverty alleviation programme in India.

(d) Discuss the various employment generation programme.

**Q. 4 Write short notes on (Any four) : (20)**

(a) e-commerce

(b) Digital economy

(c) Recent banking trends

(d) Procedure and operation of accounts

(e) Types of mergers and acquisitions

(f) Measurement of poverty.

***

www.ingramcontent.com/pod-product-compliance
Lightning Source LLC
LaVergne TN
LVHW082345171026
850499LV00040B/1338
* 9 7 8 9 3 8 9 6 8 6 4 7 0 *